AVAILABLE TITLES

ASITPLEASESGOD.COM

COURAGE

THE VALLEY CANNOT STOP GREATNESS; IT PREPARES YOU!

Copyright © 2024 by R.O.A.R. Publishing Group. All rights reserved.

Visit www.RoarPublishingGroup.com for more information. No part of this publication may be reproduced, stored in a retrieval system, or transmitted in any way by any means, electronic, mechanical, photocopy, recording, or otherwise, without the prior permission of the author except as provided by USA copyright law.

R.O.A.R. Publishing Group
581 N. Park Ave. Ste. #725
Apopka, FL 32704
ROAR-58-2316
762-758-2316
www.RoarPublishingGroup.com

Published in the United States of America
ISBN: 978-1-948936-84-2
$22.88

PLEASE SEND PRAYERS, TESTIMONIES, DONATIONS, OR ORDERS TO:

Dr. Y. Bur
R.O.A.R. Publishing Group
581 N. Park Ave. Ste. #725
Apopka, FL 32704
ROAR-58-2316
762-758-2316
✉ Dr.YBur@gmail.com

Visit Us At:
@AsItPleasesGodMovement
▶ AsItPleasesGod

🖥 DrYBur.com
🖥 AsItPleasesGod.com

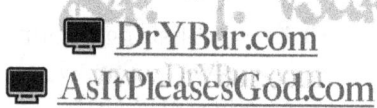

Please DONATE to this *Missionable Movement of God* as a GIVE-BACK to the Kingdom. Thanks for your support. Many Blessings.

AIPG Donation Link

Scan to Pay

Table of Contents

Introduction 7
Chapter One 15
   Spiritual Awareness 15
Chapter Two 27
   Symbolic Testimony 27
Chapter Three 41
   Love, Joy, and Happiness 41
Chapter Four 49
   Weapons of Hope 49
Chapter Five 65
   Spiritual Weapons 65
Chapter Six 73
   Second Wind of Faith 73
Chapter Seven 85
   Standing Our Ground 85
Chapter Eight 97
   Yoke Breaker 97
Chapter Nine 123
   Clean Playing 123
Chapter Ten 137
   Hidden Gift 137
Chapter Eleven 155
   Courage 155

Chapter Twelve..175
    Unveiled Queries...175

INTRODUCTION

As we look upon our current day situations, we must ask ourselves, 'Can we really take life seriously, especially when tomorrow is not promised to anyone?' Then again, we may also ask, 'Do we have the COURAGE to move forward, especially when there are seemingly no benefits in doing so?' The questions we secretly ask and openly unawaringly act upon are not coincidental. Actually, in the Eye of God, they are indeed evolutional, filled with Divine Revelation. In this book, *Courage*, we are provided another lens from a Spiritual Perspective to Divinely Illuminate the paths and Divinely Extract the Wisdom hidden in plain sight. For those who are determined to Grow Great in and out of the Kingdom of God, with this book, they will not miss a beat.

Amid all of the peaks and valleys, as Dr. Y. Bur, The Why Doctor, and according to the Heavenly of Heavens, it has given me my Divinely Blueprinted REASON and PLATFORM to do what I do best. God has given me the ability to answer the WHY questions, bringing TRUTH and LIGHT to everyone, from the pews to the pulpits and beyond, releasing the COURAGE needed to take us to the next level, *As It Pleases Him*.

I can attest that the Promises of God are real, not just for one person, but for all of us, especially if we dare to take the time to truly understand the Spiritual Principles set in place for our benefit. With all due respect, when we lack the understanding of how to apply Kingdom Principles to our daily lives, we will find ourselves in a constant loop of unanswered questions and vilified dilemmas.

Personally, I was one of those who lacked the understanding as well, and I am not ashamed to admit I did not know. Nor did I understand the underlying Spiritual Prerequisites I needed in order to possess what rightly belonged to me. As a result, I suffered many losses, mishaps, missteps, setbacks, and battle scars due to the lack of understanding of what I needed to contend with the Wiles of the Enemy.

Fortunately, some of the warring experiences were self-induced due to bad decisions, disobedience, conditioning, lack of understanding, and as an innocent, naive bystander in Spiritual Training for such a time as this. Here is what the Spiritual Classroom taught me about what needed to be done for the Kingdom of God:

- ☐ In my *Spiritual Valley* phase, I was laughed at for my Walk with God. As a result, by focusing on being in Purpose on purpose, it Spiritually Sealed my tenacity to move forward in the Will of God by any means necessary.

- ☐ In my *Spiritual Egypt and Developmental* phase, I was made fun of and bullied for my idiosyncrasies. Amid all this, it taught me how to be unique in my Giftings, Calling, Talents, Purpose, and Creativity, doing what most are not willing to do. More importantly, it positioned me to move forward in the Spirit of Excellence with my flaws with a work-in-progress mentality.

- ☐ In my *Spiritual Wandering* phase, I was ridiculed for establishing a Spiritual Zone of peace to tune into the Voice of God. In this nomadic place, following Divine Instructions from the Heavenly of Heavens trained me to develop my *Spirit to Spirit* Connection to Spiritually See, Hear, Speak, and Answer the questions that most cannot.

- ☐ In my *Promised Land* phase, I was degraded, abused, and used for my humility. Whereas, in all actuality, it was my hidden ammunition of strength in disguise, giving me Kingdom Leverage and Divine Favor. Meanwhile, my mockers were operating on worldly pompousness for the favor of man and selling out to the highest bidder.

In the carnality of it all, I was given a Promise from God that if I followed His Divine Lead, taking heed to the Spiritual Instructions given, He would heal me in ways that would put my enemies and naysayers in awe. At the same time, doing for me what money cannot buy. What is more, He has not disappointed me, nor has He reneged on His Promise.

With Divine Courage from the Heavenly of Heavens, as I lead by example, *As It Pleases God*, with this book, I hold nothing back. What is more, I am giving everyone the same opportunity to experience what God has done and is still doing within me. As my *Give-Back* to the Kingdom, I share my documentation and findings with others as my *Symbolic Testimony*, helping others to Spiritually See, Hear, and Speak according to their Divine Blueprint and *As It Pleases God*.

Our highest and greatest potential lies within, waiting for the right moment to come forth as pure gold; yet, we must know and understand the proper protocol for releasing our true Genius capabilities. Unbeknown to most, amid our underlying Courage, there are a lot of hidden Gifts, Talents, Callings, and Creativity going unnoticed and severely compromised due to our lack of understanding. For this reason, it is imperative to usher in some form of *Spiritual Awareness* to get our wheels turning in the correct direction or to become appropriately balanced, *As It Pleases God*.

Although rising out of the ashes or valley is a process, we have everything we need to continue, complete, and pursue, even if it appears as if we are on our last leg or are overlooked.

In the Kingdom, there is a Time and a Season for everything. When we are out of Season, or the timing is not right, it is imperative to be in Spiritual Training for the next SEASON, while Spiritually Tilling (Cultivating) our own ground. By availing ourselves to the Promises of God in this manner, it is Spiritually Designed to bring us in Purpose on purpose, with an understanding of our *What, When, Where, Why, How,* and with *Whom* Spiritual Truths, *As It Pleases God.*

According to the Heavenly of Heavens, a valley cannot stop Divine Greatness. Regardless of how deep or shallow it is, it is designed to PREPARE us for what is next. As *God Promised* to deliver, He has not failed in Spiritually Unveiling the Veiled, but we must extend our capacity to receive, *As It Pleases Him.* If not, the Spiritual Veil will remain until we come to ourselves or awaken from our slumber.

As a poignant illustration, if someone gives us something, and we reach out to receive it with our hands closed, it is impossible to freely take possession of what they are giving us, right? Whereas the same principle applies to the Promises of God, He is pouring into us, but the question remains, 'Are we receiving?' 'Do we really want it?' 'Are we playing in His face?' Or, 'Are we secretly pimping or prostituting Him to get what we want?' Even though in our Spiritual Journey of Faith, these questions may seem a little taxing, daunting, or irrelevant, our heart and mind postures say what we cannot articulate openly. Whereas in this book, *Courage,* we are up for the challenge, promoting rich inner dialogue, *Spirit to Spirit.*

Our Divine Overflow or Abundance is predicated on using our extraordinary capabilities already within. Once again, it will take *Courage* to unveil, possess, or release them, *As It Pleases God.* In gaining a deeper understanding of all things Spiritual, if one desires mediocrity, then this book may not be for them. Why not? We must expose our *Unveiled Queries* of WHY we are settling for being ordinary, mainly when our Divine Blueprint contains extraordinarily unique commodities. So, if we are not ready for real change, then it is best to leave the Spiritual Aspects of Divine Evolution alone.

In the pursuit of excellence, *As It Pleases God,* if we are at a standstill, in doubt, or in conflict from within, then it is imperative to uproot, regraft, or remove the harmful debris blocking us. Doing so will stretchably teach, train, and mold us in the Kingdom's Approach to Growing Greater, capitalizing on our Grandeur Possibilities, and *Standing Our Ground* for what rightly belongs to us. As we navigate our Spiritual Journeys, regardless of whether we feel deserving or not, this innate desire lies within everyone, and we all have *Hidden Gifts*. Yes, that is right! No one is exempt! In the Eye of God, it is just a matter of how much harmful debris is blocking our inner-born Genius, zapping our *Courage*, or our level of desire to become a *Yoke Breaker*, releasing our *Hidden Gifts* from captivity.

In this book, *Courage* is NOT the absence of fear or lack of faith. It is the ability to keep moving in the Spirit of Excellence, doing what we were called to do amid doubt, fear, and faith lapses. Really? Yes, really! Our enemies will shoot their shots, and if we fall short, we must be willing to get back up again. In the Eye of God, our *Courage* is a MANIFESTATION of our faith and hope in action. Unfortunately, without actionable use for the just and unjust alike, our *Courage* can become stunted.

Here is a noteworthy example: I have had many people approach me, boasting about how courageous, successful, wealthy, and astute they were, but they lacked faith in God and did not make a secret about it. In addition, they were also full of doubt about who they were and could not hit a lick at a crooked stick when it came down to Spiritual Power and Authority. But one thing is for sure, they had faith in their money, they did not doubt their cash flow, and they had the courage to outdo anyone who had less than them, including Believers serving God Almighty.

How is it possible to lack faith, especially when it takes some sort of faith to become successful, wealthy, or astute? In the Eye of God, faith is faith. Whether we believe in Mammon or God, it will work if we work it. The Spiritual Principles from the Beginning of Time do not discriminate like we do. Respectfully speaking, is this not why worldly individuals are circling hoops around Believers when it comes to the Wealth Commodity? We as Believers must develop the *Courage* to change the Wealth

Trajectory. How so? By using all the Spiritual Principles, *As It Pleases God*, and not half of them to please ourselves.

Conversely, bragging is indeed a form of insecurity, which is a lack of faith once the layers are peeled back! Although from the above story, they had a few Spiritual Principles right regarding their wealth, they also had a few wrong regarding their character. Here is what Proverbs 27:2 advises: "*Let another man praise you, and not your own mouth; a stranger, and not your own lips.*" To add insult to injury, after asking fact-finding questions, I dug a little deeper into the psyche. Listed below is a compilation of the common profiles that continued to occur:

- ☐ They were negative.
- ☐ They used others to get things done for free.
- ☐ Their people skills sucked.
- ☐ They refused to remain on a learning curve continually.
- ☐ They were critical of others appearing beneath them.
- ☐ They possessed all types of rotten fruit.
- ☐ They lacked self-control.
- ☐ They buckled under pressure with anger, rage, or abuse.
- ☐ They did not like being told what to do.

Although I had to remain respectful and polite for each encounter, I still thought to myself, 'What type of courage is this?' 'Are they not ashamed to brag about refusing to become better, stronger, and wiser?' 'Do they not have real friends to encourage them to work on themselves, positively?' Surely, someone should have informed them that money, influence, and prestige cannot buy good character. It is developed!

Are we not allowed to have our braggadocious moments, especially when working hard? Absolutely! We all deserve our moments to celebrate our accomplishments. Interwoven in this analysis, keep in mind that in the Eye of God, *Courage* and bragging are like archenemies! Really? Yes, really! Please allow me to share what James 4:16 has to say about this: "*But now you boast in your arrogance. All such boasting is evil.*"

It does not matter where we are in life or with whom, if we give credit to God or His Kingdom, then it changes the trajectory of our moments, whether good, bad, or indifferent. Here is how to approach this matter, *As It Pleases God*: "*But of Him you are in Christ Jesus, who became for us wisdom from God—and righteousness and sanctification and redemption— that, as it is written, 'He who glories, let him glory in the Lord.'*" 1 Corinthians 1:30-31.

We must face *Courage*, fear, faith, hope, or whatever head-on, *As It Pleases God*. I must admit, to do so requires strength, determination, and a willingness to take risks. Exhibiting *Courage, As It Pleases Him*, we can overcome our doubts, hangups, and insecurities with unwavering faith and hope, making us Kingdomly Usable.

According to the Heavenly of Heavens, the '*Good, Better, Best, to Greatest*' is in our nature. Suppose we do not understand and use our Gifts, Talents, and Creativity according to our Divine Blueprint. In this case, we will find ourselves becoming extremely competitive, playing dirty to stimulate or simulate this feeling. Whereas, in this Book, *Courage: As It Pleases God*, I am paving the way on how to use *Clean Playing* as a form of Spiritual Leverage, taking our '*Good, Better, Best, to Greatest*' desires from competitiveness to Righteousness, and then handing the Spiritual Mantle to another to do likewise.

On this Spiritual Journey, no one will have the exact same experiences. Plus, due to our Predestined Blueprint, there are no ready-made, A-B-C, 1-2-3, or 1-Way formulas in the Promises of God. However, there are step-by-step processes helping us to gain leverage or build momentum, but they are not set in stone.

Why does God avoid rudimentary plans? He is training us to become CORNERSTONES, *As It Pleases Him*, with the use of stepping stones. From experience, we may not know the stepping stone until we get to it. For this reason, we must develop our Spiritual Senses and Instincts to think on our feet or stay on ready. While simultaneously getting rid of the kryptonic habits, having the potential to cause any form of Spiritual Paralysis or Error.

When living by example while setting the pace for another, it is imperative to elevate and build instead of degrading and breaking down. With this in mind, if we master the conversion of negatives into positives, building positive relationships filled with *Love, Joy, and Happiness*, it gives us the legitimate right to use the Spiritual Weapons, including the *Weapons of Hope*, supplying us with our *Second Wind of Faith*.

So, if you are ready to get started on your Courage Journey, let us go deeper into the Realm of the Spirit, releasing the most extraordinary gift known to man, which is the Power of being YOU.

Dr. Y. Bur

www.DrYBur.com

Chapter One

SPIRITUAL AWARENESS

Spiritual Awareness is empowering, but more importantly, it is Divinely Liberating. It helps us develop our Personal Power in ways most do not understand. Yet, it makes us humble enough to allow others to want to cooperatively understand 'What' makes us tick and 'Why' we do what we do. What would cause this to happen? It is the *Gravitational Pull* or the positive flow of energy from the Heavenly of Heavens residing within us, commonly referred to as our Heaven on Earth Experience.

We often do not speak about our Heaven on Earth Experience because we think it is a bunch of hoopla or a money-making prosperity tactic. The truth is, most often, we do not have this Divine Experience because we are stuck on the negative without realizing it. Really? Yes, really! In a collective effort to unveil the truth, what I have found is that negativity is often misunderstood, underestimated, or overrated.

As a part of our human nature, we all know right from wrong; yet, if our conscience takes a back seat, we become inadvertently reckless, dull, pompous, stiff-necked, and disobedient to please ourselves. Plus, selfishness will close our eyes to the elements of negativity, where we appear right in our own eyes. Frankly, according to the Heavenly of Heavens, once we become accustomed to this sort of behavior, negativity slips through the cracks, depositing the Seeds of Negativity into our Mind, Body, and Soul. Then, after we are completely yoked, soul-tied, or oppressed, it seeps into other areas of our lives, contaminating everything and everyone. Sadly, this cycle will continue in our Bloodline unless we make a conscious effort to stop or counteract it. How? It finds a way to wreak havoc Mentally and Emotionally, secretly binding the human psyche into knots of debauchery by default.

In the developmental process of our Spiritual Self, we must also understand that we are unique in our own right. Why do we need to know this about ourselves? To truly master the self-enriched abilities, skills, talents, and creativity we already possess, we must KNOW they exist, or we must come into an AWARENESS of them. The truth is, we can all put up a superficial façade, hiding behind the talents of another or gleaning where we have not sown; however, the goal is to illuminate what is hidden in plain sight within the human psyche. What would this be? The real person behind the mask!

According to the Heavenly of Heavens, regardless of whether we are in a secret or open battle with ourselves or others, we have the right to invoke peace from within, safeguarding our souls. What is the purpose of demanding peace? If we do not put a demand on it, the uproaring within the human psyche has enough power to drive us seemingly insane, wreak havoc, ruin our character, and disrupt our people skills. More importantly, it will also create an illusion of us having it all together, fooling our counterparts, when there is no trace of Spiritual Solitude or Solidarity in sight.

For the most part, if we are not aware of what is going on from within, we will find ourselves cluelessly running from pillar to post without any form of healing or understanding. What do we need to do to become Spiritually Aware of who we are from the inside out?

As It Pleases God®: Book Series

- ☐ We must understand and acknowledge our core Belief System, preferably a Heavenly One; however, we must decide for ourselves.

- ☐ We must make a conscious decision to Spiritually Awaken ourselves from our state of slumber.

- ☐ We must determine 'What' we want in life. We must also define When, Where, How, and Why we want it as well. From experience, this is best done through Journaling or Mind Mapping daily to extract what is covered by layers of hidden debris, traumas, or biases. It also helps us to avoid pilfering the hard work of another, allowing us to put in the work for ourselves, giving us confidence and staying power in our Divine Calling.

- ☐ We must put away the lies we are telling ourselves and others, sustaining our superficial mask.

- ☐ We must pinpoint our internal and external motives, adjusting them to the positive side of the spectrum.

- ☐ We must determine our direction of focus or level of distractions, fine-tuning them accordingly to create a win-win.

- ☐ We must consider 'What' we think of ourselves and others, as well as the reasons 'Why' we allow ourselves to reflect in such a manner. Doing so helps us make the appropriate adjustments or corrections needed to maintain a Positive and Fruitful Mindset.

- ☐ We must account for our daily 'Give-Back' into the Kingdom for the conveyance of whatever and whomever we value.

- ☐ We must become cognizant of our habits, lusts, weaknesses, vices, and kryptonite, allowing ourselves to become a work-in-progress to avoid a Mental, Physical, Emotional, or Spiritual Derailment when we least expect it.

- ☐ We must become ever so willing to right our wrongs, repent, forgive, let go, and have mercy on ourselves and others. Doing so helps us to allow our mishaps, flaws, or mistakes to make us cohabitantly better without becoming indecisively bitter, particularly as the Vicissitudes of Life continue with or without our permission.

- ☐ We must be willing to learn amid all things without becoming rude, disobedient, abrasive, confrontational, defensive, and combative, disrupting our Personal Power or Spiritual Growth.

- ☐ We must become humble, exhibiting the Fruits of the Spirit and Christlike Character, especially when we are thrown a curveball to distract us or create an imbalance within the human psyche. More importantly, becoming humble helps us to love ourselves and others without trying to control or place them in some form of bondage. Unbeknown to most, *Unconditional Love* bridges the gap in humanity in ways unknown to the human psyche. On the other hand, conditions create yokes, bondage, and enslavement, causing inner rebellion or secret vendettas. So, beware!

Spiritual Awareness is sought by all and misunderstood by most. Those around us condition us, and if we are not Spiritually Rooted, some form of defamation or deformation will occur due to our lack of exposure or understanding. However, all is not lost; this book is designed to set the record straight, Spiritually Regrafting the Mind, Body, Soul, and Spirit according to the Heavenly Standards set forth by the King of Kings and the Lord of Lords, *As It Pleases Him.*

We can tiptoe around what we have learned through our life's journey. However, in the Eye of God, if we have not tapped into the Spiritual Elements of the Great Unknown, we still have work to do. Why do we still need to put in the work? Unbeknown to most, we are Spirit first, having a human experience. If we put our earthly experiences before our Heaven on Earth Experiences, we will encounter a Spiritual Upset or a Void from within.

When we cover our Spirit with layers of harmful debris, the human psyche becomes weighed down. Of course, therapy helps to remove the unwanted elements of debris, and it helps us understand it as well. However, without interjecting the natural design of Spirituality, we remove one negative thing and replace it with another negative or seemingly positive, with zero understanding of our Spiritual Genetic Makeup. As a result of this form of omission, it creates a Spiritual Trap, a Catch-22, or a Mocking or Judgmental Spirit.

To say the least, life can become a little complex at times, especially when life is lifing and we are clueless about our next move or what God is doing. Nevertheless, when extending *Courage* during these times, it can leave us feeling overwhelmed and confused, but we must remain focused.

According to the Heavenly of Heavens, life in itself is designed to work in our favor, especially if we begin to understand and RESPECT the Cycle of Life in totality. What does the Cycle of Life have to do with our existence? We were created from the dust of the earth, thus connecting us to the Cycles, Seasons, and Vicissitudes of Life by default.

In reality, animals have less, living in seemingly atrocious conditions, but they are more connected to God than we are. From my perspective, they have to trust Him for everything, including life, while standing on guard at all times. Listed below are a few things I have noticed about them:

- ☐ They do not complain, bicker, fuss, or fight with God about their existence.

- ☐ They protect their Bloodline.

- ☐ They use their instincts to survive, fighting for their right to live.

- ☐ They pay attention to their surroundings to avoid annihilation.

- ☐ They adapt accordingly, doing what it takes to regenerate against all odds.

- ☐ They make the most of what they have or their habitat.

- ☐ They are happy with who they are and where they live.

- ☐ They never question why they are operating in the role granted to them.

- ☐ They eat according to their Divine Design.

- ☐ They do not go on all types of diets to be a certain size or to fit in a certain clique.

- ☐ They grow, learn, and do more, building their stability, agility, and strength according to how God created them. What is the purpose of doing so? According to the Cycle of Life, it is designed to take out the weak, feeble, or disobedient, making them easy prey. In my opinion, this is really where the '*Strong Survive.*'

- ☐ They develop their own mastery, boggling the human mind to outsmart us, especially when we think we have them all figured out. How is this possible? For example, they instinctively learn our language. Thus, we have yet to learn their communicable dialect, so we can only speculate.

Animals are animals, and humans will be humans, right? The truth is, we have been Spiritually Blessed with more. Up till now, we find ourselves doing less with the Gifts of Life, especially with our Spiritual Instincts and Insight. At times, if we are truly honest with ourselves, as it relates to our human nature, we will also find ourselves giving a rat's tail about anything or anyone outside of us.

Why do we behave selfishly? Unfortunately, this mainly happens when the Fruits of the Spirit and Christlike Character are not appropriately used, or we have become openly or secretly abused, used, victimized, or traumatized by something or someone.

What is the big deal, especially when we have all experienced the Vicissitudes of Life? Abuse, victimization, and trauma are the leading causes of unused or underutilized Gifts, Calling, Talents, and Creativity. Why? The human psyche is very fickle and controlling. Plus, it tends to rehash whatever will keep us under control or allow it to remain in charge, beating us down from the inside out with negativity, fear, or a simulation of defeat. What does this mean? The Spiritual Connection of Oneness with the Holy Spirit cannot take place with our soulish nature being in charge of our Mind, Body, and Soul.

How can our soulish nature control us, especially when we are devout Believers? It does not matter if we are Believers or not; our soulish nature will oppress us under the victimized guise of pointing the finger as if someone is doing something to us. Or, we may become conditioned to making excuses by saying, 'It is the Devil,' or 'The Devil made me do it.' When, in all actuality, we are doing whatever it is to ourselves due to our perception, without backing whatever we are feeling with what is truthful, factual, and positive. Frankly, in my opinion, this is how we ruin the lives of the innocent to appease a soulish vendetta that appears real. For this reason, we must exercise extreme caution when spreading or engaging in false propaganda, mockery, debauchery, or judgment.

When we begin to point the finger judgmentally, we must note that we have three fingers pointing back at us. For this reason, self-examination is critical, preventing us from creating a bed of debauchery, contaminating our Bloodline or stunting our growth in or out of the Kingdom of Heaven. Why do we need to know this information? According to the Heavenly of Heavens, our daily walk in Spirituality is real, becoming more relevant than what we see with the naked eye. But, at the same time, it also holds the keys to our peaceful sanity and *Divine Courage*.

In the Eye of God, it is imperative to engage in the Spiritual Reformation Process when it comes down to our *Spiritual Awareness*. What is the purpose of doing so? It helps to bring us into Oneness with our Heaven on Earth Experience instead of instigating division in a superfluous reality of our own making. Besides, it reduces the risk of having the Cycle of Life take us out or zap our Personal Power due to some form of weakness, vulnerability, disobedience, or derision. To be clear, I do not wish this upon anyone...so let us take this a step further, *As It Pleases God*.

Henceforth, we must be 'In The Know' regarding how the Kingdom of Heaven selects and dethrones, *As It Pleases God*. Why must we know this? It is essential for those who OMIT using the Fruits of the Spirit and Christlike Character as a Spiritual Platform or Weapon of Warfare. Can we really become dethroned as Believers, especially when we are not on a Throne? Absolutely. The Throne of God is WITHIN, and if we are oblivious to this Spiritual Fact, we can 'get got' or turn on ourselves without knowing it.

According to the Heavenly of Heavens, we become a magnet, creating a Spiritual Gravitational Pull inwardly by what we extend outwardly and vice versa. What if we are not a magnet? Although we have free will, unfortunately, we do not have a choice in this matter. Once we were created from the dust of the earth, we were GRANDFATHERED into the Law of Gravity.

Particularly, if we have not mastered the Spiritual Cleansing Process, we must be very cautious. What is the purpose of such caution? Compounded negativity becomes our inner kryptonite, spreading outwardly. Now, to avoid this, we must master the process of releasing the negative back into its original state, counteracting it with some form of positivity to maintain our State of Balance, Neutralness, or Tranquility, *As It Pleases God*.

What is the purpose of counteracting negatives with positives? If negativity remains without a positive counteraction, we become imbalanced by default. For example, if the pH balance in our hair is off, it creates an imbalance leading to unhealthiness within the hair's root, spreading outwardly to the hair shaft. If not rectified accordingly, in due time, this imbalance will eventually display our inner condition outwardly for all to see. In addition, it will outright affect the growth of our hair on a sliding scale, determining what we can or cannot do with our hair.

With the pH sliding scale, the improperly gauged oil flow in the hair follicle will cause our hair to become too oily, weighing it down or causing limpness. In contrast, the lack of it causes it to become too brittle, resulting in some form of breakage. Yet, amid all, in doing our part in counteracting a negative with a positive in our hair's pH balance, regulating it between 4.5 to 5.5, our hair is then adequately equipped to do the rest; or better yet, it will heal itself.

Now, from a Spiritual Perspective, when it comes down to our Spiritual Oil, for it to flow effectively and succinctly, our Spiritual pH System must become adequately balanced as well. Why? It gives us an indication when an imbalance is causing a derailment, we are becoming ineffectively limp, we are on the verge of breaking down, or we are too abrasive in our approach. How insulting is it to compare our hair with all things Spiritual, right? In all due respect, what is coming out of our head is just as important as the head itself.

Moreover, our hair is a part of our body with many members; therefore, the same pH Principles applying to our bodily functions that cause them to work together for our good also apply to our Spiritual Functions. Our pH is basically a system used to keep us in check; therefore, we cannot omit what is Divinely Designed to work in our favor, especially if we simply pay attention without developing a deaf ear. Also, when dealing with our Spiritual Crown, the head is the only member of the body we will place the Mark of Royalty or Spiritual Seal, *As It Pleases God*. Thus, if we understand the head, the body will follow!

On the other hand, if we become self-defiant, selfish, or lack self-control while outright negating Spiritual Truths, this cliché will apply: *'If we kill the head, the body dies by default.'* For this reason, to those who willfully neglect their Spiritual Crowns, the Heavenly of Heavens is calling for us to do better.

How can we do better, *As It Pleases God*? First, it is done by making a conscious decision to protect the HEAD. Secondly, we must set a guard over our Mind, Body, and Soul with the help of the Holy Spirit. Thirdly, we must plead the Blood of Jesus in all things while repenting, forgiving, praying, and giving thanks daily. Why do we need to go to such an extent? Without it, in time, all else fails! Besides, human intervention cannot contend with Divine Intervention, *As It Pleases God*. So, it is always best to approach life from a Spiritual Perspective to avoid creating a deficit within oneself.

To Spiritually Absorb all God has for us, we must be willing to open the Gateway of Wisdom, allowing the Heavenly Oil to flow to and through us, reaching the intended targets. Unfortunately, the moment we become close-minded, we cut the flow, becoming temporarily unusable in the Eye of God with a symbolic *'Out of Service'* sign on our foreheads.

When disconnected from the Source, we then rely on ourselves to do what is intended to be Divine. Once this happens, the ego takes over, causing us to engage when we should be disengaging. How do we recognize when we are becoming self-reliant?

- [ ] We must take note of our motives, whether they are good, bad, indifferent, or self-seeking.

- [ ] We must determine if we have prayed, repented, or given thanks.

- [ ] We must decide if we have asked for Divine Intervention from the Holy Spirit.

- [ ] We must take into account how we are going about doing what we are doing. Are we deceitful, sneaky, vindictive, conniving, envious, devious, and the list goes on with negative character traits?

- [ ] We must search the heart for the secret elements of jealousy, envy, coveting, competitiveness, contention, or unforgiveness.

- [ ] We must decide if we are using the Fruits of the Spirit and exhibiting Christlike Character in our endeavors.

- [ ] We must consider whether we are acting in humility or pompousness.

- [ ] We must become aware of how we respond or react, determining if we are respectful or disrespectful in our approach.

- [ ] We must determine if we are genuinely helping others or using, abusing, or mistreating them for selfish gain.

- ☐ We must become aware of whether or not we create an environment of non-stressing harmony or a chaotic, stressful, and confusing one.

- ☐ We must know if we are leading by example positively or if we are leading people astray.

- ☐ We must be honest about whether or not we truly love ourselves from the inside out.

What is the purpose of knowing this information? Our unification process begins when we can ask fact-finding questions while honestly answering them to keep us in a *Spiritual Wave of Learning*. If not, we become prone to self-instigated biases and irrelevant conditioning, affecting those we come in contact with, similar to having a contagious virus or cold.

If our *Spiritual Immune System* is not strong enough to fight off viruses or germs, we inadvertently become affected and infected. Without realizing it, we may repeat the same pattern with others or even infect ourselves and our Bloodline repeatedly. With this in mind, *Spiritual Awareness* is definitely needed for our sake, for the sake of the ones we love, and for the sake of others to ensure our *Symbolic Testimonies* will represent the Kingdom of Heaven, *As It Pleases God*.

Chapter Two

SYMBOLIC TESTIMONY

Our greatest and highest potentials are attainable, mainly if we maximize our ability to become and remain positive while communicating effectively. According to the Heavenly of Heavens, our experiences in life are a *Symbolic Testimony* for others to learn and grow stronger, wiser, and more astute. As we all know, we are a Living Testimony; however, we are required to take it a step further for our sake. We are Representatives of the Kingdom of Heaven, who are required to 'Give-Back' to others positively, consistently, and faithfully with the Fruits of the Spirit and Christlike Character while developing our Astuteness of Divine Wisdom.

On the other side of being a Living Testimony, the compilation of our lives can indeed become negative, indifferent, rude, critical, judgmental, and disrespectful without the Holy Trinity, *As It Pleases God*. How is this possible, especially as Believers? Our actions, reactions, words, deeds, or demeanor can seem positive to the natural eye with good intentions, but our fruits are rotten. We are mean as a junkyard dog, rude as an evil stepmother, loud as a bullhorn, putting everyone on blast, and initiating contention in the Name of Jesus.

For this reason, according to Kingdom Standards, we are called to internally examine ourselves before presenting ourselves in a Kingdomly Image, especially when we are secretly or openly yoked, soul-tied, oppressed, stressed, or traumatized. What is the purpose of exercising extreme caution? If the Fruits of the Spirit and Christlike Character are not used, we will transfer negative energy into the lives of others without realizing what we are doing or with seemingly good intentions. Furthermore, this is why we must convert negatives into positives instantly, preventing the transfer of negativity.

As a Word to the Wise, according to the Heavenly of Heavens, we should extend peacefulness and harmony everywhere we place the soles of our feet. When operating in the Spirit of Excellence, if we are not careful, the sliding scale of our communicable efforts has a way of painting a superficial façade to create a sense of awe, instead of allowing us to become openly transparent regarding our reality. Why is this so important? We are a mirror, causing others to secretly or openly emulate us. As a *Symbolic Testimony* in the lives of others, if we are sharing fakeness, superficialities, or cliffhangers, others will follow suit based on their perception of our untruths.

When dealing with *Courage* in the Eye of God, a harmonious demeanor is sought after by many, yet misunderstood by most. So, it behooves us to up the ante in this area, ensuring our *A-Game* does not become our *B-Game*. Unbeknown to most, this is when we are operating beneath our Divine Gifting of Greatness encapsulated in our win-win. Only to become subservient to a lesser game, resulting in some form of loss in due time.

Listen, a sweet soul is the breeding ground for a *Symbolic Testimony*, leaving desirable imprints on the hearts of all we come in contact with. Once again, the human psyche is indeed fickle, yet it can recognize a GENUINE SPIRIT, regardless of our biases, conditioning, or level of denial. How do we know if we are on the right track with our *Symbolic Testimony*? Listed below is a small compilation of a few indicators, but not limited to such:

- ☐ When we know and understand 'Who' is in charge of our lives and 'Why,' as well as 'What' we believe.
- ☐ When we are able to own our truth, we debunk all forms of deception with the Word of God.
- ☐ When our word becomes our bond, we set a guard over our tongues.
- ☐ When we become humble and respectful to all.
- ☐ When we become consciously transparent.
- ☐ When our soulish nature is honing in on being peacefully patient.
- ☐ When we learn to love without conditions or biased favoritism.
- ☐ When we are able to use the Fruits of the Spirit, exhibiting Christlike Character, without giving it a second thought.
- ☐ When we are able to speak life into another without putting them in the grave Mentally, Physically, Emotionally, or Spiritually.
- ☐ When we are able to convert negatives into positives to create a win-win.
- ☐ When we become astute in the Spirit of Oneness.
- ☐ When we pride ourselves on becoming obedient, trainable, understanding, and commissionable.

With these indicators, we can pinpoint if we are on the right track to becoming a Representative of the Kingdom. Are we not all Representatives of the Kingdom? We all have the potential; however, if we are misrepresenting the Kingdom in any way, shape, or form, we do not need anyone to decide our fate for us. Why? According to the Heavenly of Heavens, we have free will to choose whatever and whomever we like, and for any reason, determining our Spiritual Portion.

Our Spiritual Portion is what we serve to ourselves, through ourselves, and with ourselves. What does our portion have to do with anything? Unbeknown to most, what we serve to others, we Symbolically Serve back to ourselves or into our Bloodline, be it positively, negatively, or indifferently.

How can we better understand 'What' we are doing, as well as 'Why' we are doing what we do? We are all different with different wants, needs, desires, conditions, traumas, and so on; therefore, nothing is set in stone. As a whole, we must better understand the Spiritual Process the Heavenly of Heavens requires from us according to our Divine Blueprint, *As It Pleases God*. What does this have to do with getting an understanding? When we become hell-bent on pointing the finger, we must also take into account the character traits that placed us in the position we are in today.

For example, if we are attracting negativity, we have to take into account the behaviors that place us in this position. Let us take this a step further on how the manifestation of our negative Seeds impacts us in ways we overlook. Plus, listed below are a few ways showing how it manipulates our *Symbolic Testimony* positively or negatively without us realizing it, but not limited to such:

- ☐ Do we think for a minute we can exhibit wretchedness without reaping the *Seeds* sown into our animosity with others?
- ☐ Do we think we can behave like a hellion on wheels without reaping the *Seeds* sown into having a hell-on-earth experience?
- ☐ Do we think we can beat people down, Mentally, Physically, Emotionally, and Spiritually without reaping the *Seeds* of a beatdown within our human psyche?
- ☐ Do we think it is conducive to use, abuse, mistreat, and deceive others without reaping the *Seeds* of betrayal?
- ☐ Do we think we can pilfer from others without reaping the *Seeds* of debauchery?
- ☐ Do we think we can disrespect others without reaping the *Seeds* of degradation?

- ☐ Do we think we can put down, oppress others, or treat them like a junkyard dog without reaping the *Seeds* of shamefulness?
- ☐ Do we think we can kill the dream of another without reaping the *Seeds* of failure?
- ☐ Do we think we can carelessly break the heart of another without reaping the *Seeds* of brokenness?
- ☐ Do we think we can make excuses without reaping the *Seeds* of deprivation?
- ☐ Do we think we can loom curses upon another without reaping the *Seeds* of waywardness?
- ☐ Do we think we can run away from the Mission of God without reaping the *Seeds* of missed opportunities?

According to the Kingdom of Heaven, our Seeds of Character are more potent than we can ever imagine, especially when we are sowing them cluelessly. Ungoverned Seeds have a way of spreading all over the place, in places they do not belong, and into the hidden crevices without a targeted mission, springing up when we least expect them. Conversely, when our Seeds of Character are governed, we can better determine if they are Godly or ungodly, altering the trajectory accordingly. For this reason, it is essential to exhibit respectful self-control, especially when dealing with the germination of our Charactorial Seeds.

What do our Charactorial Seeds have to do with our *Symbolic Testimony*? We become a Symbol of our Seeds. How is this possible? We are known by our Fruits. Please allow me to Spiritually Align: *"You will know them by their fruits. Do men gather grapes from thornbushes or figs from thistles?"* Matthew 7:16.

In order to get to the Fruitful aspects of anything, it must be presented or sown as a Seed first. In my opinion, the germination taking place within the human psyche is no joke! We can tiptoe around this matter all we like, but our present state of being says all, even if we are in denial or on our *'soap box'* from the past.

What causes this to happen? Whether we are sowing conscious or unconscious Seeds, we are accountable. It does not matter whether or not it is for a targeted process; we are required to know 'What' we are in, 'Why' we are in it, 'Where' we are going with it, 'How' it will benefit us, 'Who' it affects, and 'When' to make a move or cease mobility. Listed below are a few processes, but not limited to such:

- ☐ The Transitional Process.
- ☐ The Regrafting Process.
- ☐ The Cleanup Process.
- ☐ The Pruning Process.
- ☐ The Weeding Process.
- ☐ The Fertilizing Process.
- ☐ The Intentionality Process.
- ☐ The Guarded Process.
- ☐ The Uprooting Process.
- ☐ The Governing Process.
- ☐ The Systematic Process.
- ☐ The Initiation Process.

Whatever we must do to positively and fruitfully safeguard our Seeds, we must do it! Why must we go through all of this for just a Seed? If we do not govern our Seeds for ourselves, then who will do it for us? My point exactly...Nobody!

According to the Heavenly of Heavens, we must be Spiritually Willing to do what it takes before the Holy Spirit will assist us in adequately governing ourselves, *As It Pleases God*. Why must we make the first move? Remember, we have free will to do whatever, whenever, however, and with whomever. What is more, the Holy Spirit will not violate or intervene if we do not initiate the Spiritual Process, especially if *Spiritual Awareness* has not taken place.

Our self-created reality depends upon us, our Seeds, and our perception, giving way to our Divine Destiny, or whether we abort the process. Regardless of the decisions made or the Seeds that are sown, it is indeed our choice to make. In my opinion, we must choose carefully and wisely, preferably with the Holy Trinity involved. But once again, heart-to-heart, it is our choice as it relates to our self-fulfilling prophecy and what we do with the results of our self-created reality.

Of course, we all want to live life on our terms, and in my opinion, there is nothing wrong with doing so. However, when embarking on the stratosphere of *Courage*, it is imperative to incorporate the Terms or Will of God, *As It Pleases Him*. Omitting God or our Divine Purpose will cause us to become enemies of God, even if we are devout Believers. Blasphemy, right? Wrong. Either we operate God's way, *As It Pleases Him*, or our way to please ourselves. Here is what we must know: "*Adulterers and adulteresses! Do you not know that friendship with the world is enmity with God? Whoever therefore wants to be a friend of the world makes himself an enemy of God.*" James 4:4.

How is this possible when we are Believers, loving God with all our hearts? When we use God for Heavenly Benefits, and the Heavenly of Heavens cannot use us to benefit the Kingdom, it indicates that we have issues taking place within our Earthen Vessels. How? We are selfishly consuming our own fruits when they are designed to be shared with others, *As It Pleases God*. As a result, we unawaringly turn on ourselves from within due to the misuse or omission of the Fruits of the Spirit.

What type of issues are we dealing with? First and foremost, it is selfishness! Secondly, disobedience. And thirdly, Spiritual Blindness, Deafness, and Muteness. It does not matter 'Who' we are, 'Why' we are, or 'What' our Spiritual Status is or is not; this Spiritual Diagnosis does not change, period! Blasphemy, right? Wrong! Spiritually, we must stop lying to ourselves about the status of our human psyche while making superficial excuses for it. Therefore, a choice must be made: "*Choose for yourselves this day whom you will serve, whether the gods which your fathers served that were on the other side of the River, or the gods of the Amorites, in whose land you dwell. But as for me and my house, we will serve the Lord."* Joshua 24:15.

The Kingdom of Heaven does not play around with one-directional movement. It requires movement similar to a body of water *FLOWING* from one to another. Regardless of whether it is an ocean, stream, river, or lake, it must flow. If not, it becomes a puddle or cesspool prone to developing some form of septic.

Listen, due to our imperfections from the Garden of Eden, we must not allow the toxins from the Vicissitudes of Life to contaminate our Seeds or Fruits, zapping our *Courage*. Why? We are the Tree of Life, contributing to the lifecycle of the next generation. Plus, we have the power to change the trajectory of anything based on our perception, mindset, and Spiritual Know-How, *As It Pleases God*.

Why must we make the necessary changes from negative to positive and from evil to good? We do not want to become the Tree of Death, negligently drawing our Bloodline into the Pit. Nor do we want to aid in contributing to a bloodbath of destructive behaviors or character.

Clearly, I am not here to point the finger at children who misbehave. According to the Heavenly of Heavens, children will be children; they emulate what they see, hear, feel, and experience. In my opinion, they are like a sponge, soaking up everything. Due to their impressionability, this is the prime reason for having someone set a positive example to mirror accordingly.

Personally, once I learned and understood the reasons 'Why' my character development was of the utmost importance, I changed for the better, helping others to do likewise. All I needed was an understanding of how to proactively apply the Fruits of the Spirit and Christlike Character in my daily life. As positive growth began to take place, I began incorporating them in my people skills under any circumstance, and not just behind closed doors.

Our *Symbolic Testimony* is our Testament living beyond us, through us. As a Believer, it forms a life of its own from the inside out, impacting the lives of those who are willing to embrace our *God-Given* abilities as we become better people with a work-in-progress mentality without having a bitter, lethargic one. For the most part, if we lack understanding in this area, as the Testamentor (The *Symbolic Testimony* Giver) or Testamentee (The *Symbolic Testimony* Receiver), it becomes easier to hold on to unforgiveness, resentfulness, hatefulness, and bitterness.

If we do not know the negative impacts associated with our Fruits or Seeds, our issues are often left unresolved or ignored, leaving people in suspense, ghosting them, or hanging on for dear life. Not realizing that reversing the negative to a positive is the way to initially leverage our feet on the ground, cutting the cord, and breaking the yoke with whatever or whomever.

What if we are not aware of our buried negativity? When dealing with negativity from the inside out, we cannot say we are not fully aware. How is it possible to say such a thing when we are clueless about what is going on within us? It is recognized in our Fruits, Seeds, Words, Thoughts, and Deeds. From my perspective, it is fair to say that we ignore them, more so than we can say we do not know. How is this possible? Listed below are a few reasons, but not limited to such:

- ☐ We know when we are out of character, angry, or hostile.
- ☐ We know when we are doing right or wrong.
- ☐ We know when we are mean, rude, hateful, or demeaning.
- ☐ We know when we are feeling jealous, envious, and outright coveting.
- ☐ We know when our mouth is a loose cannon, breaking, corrupting, or destroying the innocent.
- ☐ We know when our thoughts are off-kilter or debauched.
- ☐ We know when we are sabotaging or killing the dreams of another.
- ☐ We know when we are reactive, defensive, chaotic, or abusive.
- ☐ We know when we are repulsive, cruel, or nasty.

- ☐ We know when we are judgmental or condescending.
- ☐ We know when we are bouncing self-destructive, negative thoughts around or entertaining negative chatter.
- ☐ We know when we are out of the Will of God, bullying people, using others, or playing the fool.

Here is the deal: We either ignore what we are doing, we do not care, we are making an excuse, we do not know how to reverse it from negative to positive, or our ego will not allow us to own our truth. The bottom line is that our *Symbolic Testimony* requires us to correct the correctable, reverse the reversible, and obey the obeyable.

We cannot run around like a hellion on wheels and think the Heavenly of Heavens will open on our behalf. Why can we not expect this to happen, especially if we are a Child of God? Once again, our *Symbolic Testimony* will rat us out! What does this mean? If we represent worldliness, we are forced to correct and repent, turning away from whatever contradicts Kingdom Authenticity.

What is the purpose of Kingdom Authenticity? The reasons may vary from person to person based on our Level of Spirituality, Correctability, or Corruptibility. What does this mean? We are all different due to our conditioning, biases, judgments, perceptions, or traumas. Therefore, we cannot determine the validity needed to obtain our Kingdom Credentials without involving the Holy Trinity. Some may require a little or a lot of tweaking; then some, like myself, may require a Spiritual Overhaul due to their Divine Mission. Yet, regardless of where we are in life, for our Kingdom Commission or the Spiritual Classroom, listed below are a few items we need to take note of, but not limited to such:

- ☐ The use of the Holy Trinity (The Father, Son, and Holy Spirit) involves God in everything.

- ☐ The use of the Fruits of the Spirit to properly govern our behavior, or the lack thereof.

- ☐ The exhibition of Christlike Character, representing what the Kingdom of Heaven expects from us as we are *Blessed to be a Blessing*.

- ☐ The ability to align ourselves and our lives with the Word of God, His Divine Principles, and His Method of Operation.

- ☐ The desire to self-correct without someone or something forcing us to do so.

- ☐ The willpower to operate in the Spirit of Righteousness, doing the right thing when no one is looking.

- ☐ The discipline to exhibit love, kindness, forgiveness, and mercy in all things without manipulating, conniving, using, or scheming.

- ☐ The capability of allowing our conscience, instincts, and intents to work on our behalf through the help of the Holy Spirit, opening our Spiritual Eyes, Ears, and Mouth.

- ☐ The agility to use the Spiritual Tools from within, such as our Spiritual Insight, Gifting, Talents, and Creativity, brings us into *Purpose on purpose*.

- ☐ The skill of Spiritual Documentation using a *Mind Map* or the *Journaling Process* to capture the Spiritual Instructions flowing from the Heavenly of Heavens.

- ☐ The prized ability to become accountable for our actions, reactions, thoughts, and desires, Mentally, Physically,

Emotionally, and Spiritually, without making excuses, playing the blaming game, or becoming a victim.

☐ The valuable *Knowledgeable Wisdom* associated with exhibiting the Power of Gratefulness in all things, regardless of how it appears to the naked eye.

Why do we need such lists? Kingdomly *Courage* is very strategic and systematic, and if we become accustomed to lists, concepts, and precepts, we can fine-tune our Spiritual Checkup from the neck up. Plus, from experience, by having an informal countdown in place, it is easier to pinpoint our point of erring, especially when the Vicissitudes of Life do not stop because we missed our cue or were unprepared.

Listen, regardless of 'Where' we are in life or 'Who' we are, life continues with or without our permission, doing what it is designed to do. Therefore, it is always best to 'Stay On Ready' at all times with the necessary information at our fingertips to refer back to, align ourselves, or reel ourselves in. It is primarily done proactively for the deterring process in our everyday living. It is also done for the distractions having the potential to cause us to do an unjustifiable or unfeasible about-face.

Then again, on a Spiritual Level, it can be used as a preventative method to avoid Mental, Physical, and Emotional booby-traps that can thwart our Spiritual Relationship with the Holy Trinity. How do we realize when this is happening? When we become fed up with something or someone, we will tend to pop off without realizing it until it is too late or we have to play clean-up. The truth of the matter is that having to play clean-up when we had the same opportunity to avoid putting ourselves in a compromising situation, feeding into the enemy's tricks, is unacceptable in the Kingdom.

When it comes down to our *Symbolic Testimony*, we must protect it from the wiles of the enemy. They will tend to put a monkey wrench in our Spiritual Impact and Foresight, causing us to second-guess ourselves. Yet, when it comes down to the Kingdom, we must humbly '*Know that we Know*' while being '*In the Know*' at the same time, as it relates to our Gifts, Calling, Talents, Creativity, Divine Destiny, or whether we are in *Purpose on Purpose*.

Why do we need to be confident? If we are wishy-washy, the enemy will hang us out to dry in Mental, Physical, Emotional, and Spiritual turmoil, causing us to question our existence or fight when we should be *Standing Tall*, while humbly standing down! What does this mean? If we are busy reacting, we have less time thinking rationally, especially when we are being provoked into foolery.

What is the big deal, primarily when we have the free will to do what we like? Frankly, if we are expecting God to BLESS intentional and unrepentant foolery, mess, or debauchery, we are sadly mistaken. The Kingdom of Heaven does not work in this manner, especially when we are causing harm to the innocent; we cannot control our thoughts or emotions, and we are easily provoked into misbehaving or becoming outright disrespectful.

Unbeknown to most, we do not have to respond to everything or everyone. If we do, people can get into our headspace, zapping our *Courage*. If we give way to this, we forfeit our Spiritual Guards governing the Sacredness of our Mental or Emotional Stability, as well as our peacefulness from within. Listen, with our *Symbolic Testimony*, we cannot allow ourselves to bounce all over the place regardless of '*What*' people think about us, the reasons '*Why*,' or whether it is justified or not.

What can we do to safeguard ourselves from instability? First, find the root cause. Secondly, repent, forgive, and bring a resolution. Then, thirdly, shake it off, give thanks, and keep it moving while staying on the positive side of the spectrum! If people choose to remain negative and condescending, let them! Candidly, if it is not our portion, we must move on to where our cup or portion overflows.

What if it does not flow? It is NOT our cup, it is NOT our portion, it is NOT our stream, or it is NOT our whatever! When we are in *Purpose on purpose*, our Spiritual Gifts, Calling, Talents, Creativity, Tools, or whatever will flow. Really? Yes, really!

If we like to waste time, we can; however, I am not in the business of wasting precious time undoing or redoing what I can get right the first time around. What is the purpose of adequately governing our time? Whatever or whomever we need is already there; we simply must know it and position ourselves accordingly, allowing our *Symbolic Testimony* to flow in the tune of the Heavenly of Heavens.

We do not want to miss our cue, throwing us into a cycle of déjà vu, a cyclone of mismanagement, or a life series of irresponsibility. What is the big deal? Carelessness and recklessness are not befitting qualities for tending the Flocks of God, nor is it conducive to the edification process without Divine Intervention or Correction. What does this mean? According to the Heavenly of Heavens, we will soon be required to step into the Spiritual Classroom for additional training in order to Spiritually Transition into Kingdom Material.

To ensure that God's sheep are treated with respect, it is necessary to adopt a gentle, humble, and consistent approach when dealing with them. Being responsible and effective in our approach is also crucial to avoid mishandling them.

For the record, God loves us all. He wants us to experience joy and happiness; therefore, He does not want us to be wounded or to become wounded beyond repair out of negligence.

As the Heavens shine upon us, *Courage* is on a silver platter for the taking, but to become truly *Symbolic*, we will be TESTED to develop our Testimony, *As It Pleases God*.

Chapter Three

LOVE, JOY, AND HAPPINESS

We all desire true Love, Joy, and Happiness, but they are truly obtained by few. We sometimes lack understanding from a Heavenly Perspective; thus, when the temporary illusion of Love, Joy, and Happiness is seemingly felt, with time, it eludes us for some reason or false expectation. What causes this to happen? First, we are Spiritual Beings, yet very relational. For this reason, we are designed to communicate effectively while consistently developing our people skills. Secondly, Love and Joy are the intangibles dwelling within us, spreading outwardly into the real world. At the same time, it grants us happiness through our sensual tangibilities with people, places, things, events, circumstances, and so on.

On the other hand, if hate, debauchery, negativity, or unrest dwells from within us, it is reflected outwardly, especially when our internal layers are peeled back when no one is looking. If we are happy about hurting, betraying, bullying, or breaking someone down, Mentally, Physically, Emotionally, and Spiritually, it is an indication that our conscience has taken a back seat. It may also mean our sensual (inner) intangibles have become desensitized, causing some form of Spiritual Blindness, Deafness, or Muteness.

What are the sensual (outer) tangibilities? They are the things we can see, feel, taste, smell, and hear. These are all designed to provoke, evoke, motivate, enlighten, satiate, traumatize, or shut down the human psyche. Truthfully, if we cannot love or experience Joy from within the human psyche, we will not experience Happiness the way God intended, nor can real *Courage* reside.

In all reality, the Fruits of the Spirit (Love, Joy, Peace, Patience, Kindness, Goodness, Faithfulness, Gentleness, and Self-Control) tell us what we need to do to experience or obtain Happiness from a Heavenly Perspective that comes with its own Spiritual Dose of *Courage*.

Yet, for some reason, the substantial value of our Spiritual Fruits eludes us, as society paints a worldly image of having money, fame, fortune, status, position, or the physicalities of life as if it is the way to obtain lasting Happiness, to become relevant, or exude *Courage*. Nonetheless, all the luxuries are nice to have; however, regardless of what we have or do not have, we are still Blessed beyond measure.

Clearly, amid living life, it will become challenging to see, understand, or recognize the Blessings hidden in plain sight when we are focused on the wrong things or faking it. Once again, having the abundance of life or living comfortably is ideal, but it is not the true origin of Love or Joy. Nor should we wrap the contingency of our Happiness in things. Listed below are a few reasons, but not limited to such:

- ☐ It will cause us to secretly or openly sell our souls to obtain material things with fleeting value.

- ☐ It will cause us to feel worthless or undervalued if we do not have the most up-to-date things to keep up with the Joneses.

As It Pleases God®: Book Series

- ☐ It will cause our perception to become off-kilter, insecure, and unstable, prompting us to look down on or brow-bash others for the same things we are secretly or openly guilty of, primarily when our hiccups in life are listed under a different label.

- ☐ It will cause us to become violent over menial, replaceable things.

- ☐ It will cause us to judge or point the finger at things we do not understand.

- ☐ It will cause us to become jealous, envious, or prideful, invoking us to go deep into debt to feel superior or maintain a particular type of fleeting image or lifestyle.

- ☐ It will cause us to covet things that are not for us, what is not a part of our Divine Blueprint, or what outright does not belong to us.

- ☐ It will cause us to cut off or overlook our Divine Blessings.

- ☐ It will cause the basis for our conscience to have little or no sense of value for human life. While simultaneously invoking the desire to eradicate those who get in the way of what we want.

- ☐ It will cause the Holy Spirit to go into a state of dormancy, as our material unrest drives our human psyche into the Abyss of turmoil or braggadociosness.

- ☐ It will cause our fruits to become spoiled rotten, oozing ungratefulness all over the place.

- ☐ It will cause us to create rifts in our people skills, destroying relationships due to our worldly personality of the *'nothing is ever good enough'* demeanor.

In all actuality, according to the Heavenly of Heavens, the true origin of real, lasting Happiness is wrapped in our Spiritual Fruits and Christlike Character. How is this possible? It helps to build Spiritual Righteousness to properly manage our health, wealth, and good success from the Heavenly of Heavens with no shame attached. What does this mean? We are Blessed to become a Blessing, not to spitefully become someone's worst nightmare or ultimate demise, doing all sorts of evil without a conscience.

Listen, we should not be afraid to use Heavenly Provisions to do good, building the Kingdom, *As It Pleases God*. However, we must exercise extreme caution when using Spiritual Provisions to conduct evil, negative, and wayward acts, tearing down the Kingdom or the Anointed Vessels of God.

What is the big deal, primarily when we work for our own provisions, having free will to do whatever we like with whomever? From a Spiritual Perspective, all things are from God. Plus, we do have free will to do whatever with whomever; nonetheless, the sources of the provision will vary. In every aspect of life, we have good sources, bad sources, evil sources, righteous sources, dark sources, shady sources, and so on.

If we value our Love, Joy, and Happiness, all I am saying is do not use Divine, Positive, Righteous, Wise, or Heavenly Sources to do evil, period! It creates generational curses, zapping our inner Joy and Happiness by default, causing us to eventually turn on ourselves due to our bouts with our perception of Love or our inner hostilities about it.

The Spiritual Interconnection of *Love, Joy,* and *Happiness* eludes most of us due to our worldly perception or conditioning. Amid our misunderstandings or misconceptions, we have many couples, families, or relationships appearing to have it all. The moment the Vicissitudes of Life avail, their staying power seems to vanish. Unfortunately, they fall apart due to some form of materialism or fighting over money, especially when they claim to love each other.

But what behooves me the most is that the once-loving individual turns into a vicious tyrant when faced with being on the losing end. According to the Heavenly of Heavens, authentic Love does not cause us to behave like this, but conditional, expectational, trophy, or purchased Love does.

In my opinion, if we want to play dirty, we should always play dirty on the dark side or with those of a like Spirit. If we use the Kingdom of God, attempting to throw shade or dig ditches for the Spiritually Righteous, in due time, we will be exposed to the Light, called out, or put on blast for Heaven's Sake. Really? Yes, really!

When we think we are above Kingdom Laws, attempting to negatively alter Heaven's Blueprint with someone who is in Purpose on purpose, we become an enemy or a footstool of the Kingdom. What does this mean? Suppose God allows the enemy to unjustifiably attack a Spiritual Elite or someone who is wholeheartedly attempting to become Righteous, *As It Pleases Him*. In this case, it is going to build them, make them better, make them more BLESSED, or drive them into the Arms of God.

On the other hand, He may shut it down altogether; no one knows the Mind of God; therefore, we should not ever get to the point where we think we are above Him, attempt to outsmart Him, or use our provisional resources to engage in debauchery.

How do we know the difference in our sources? When dealing with our provisional resources, the difference is usually found in how they are obtained, the motives behind them, and how we are using them. All of our reasonings in life are intertwined in our 'What' and 'Why' factors.

The moment we can fine-tune our *Q and A Sessions* with ourselves, it will begin to *Spiritually Unveil* the valuable information needed to correct the correctable, bear the seemingly unbearable, understand what we misunderstood, break the limits where we were once limited, and so on. Once we become open to this form of Spiritual Classroom, the *'How To'* will avail itself, as the Holy Spirit will guide us to the *'Where To'* and *'With Whom'* we should deal with or shut down.

Clearly, no one will experience outward happiness 100% of the time. Something will indeed disgust us from time to time, but we can exhibit Love or Joy as a chosen state of being 100% of the time. What does this mean? We cannot govern what takes place around us, but we can govern what is happening within us. How do we go about doing so? We must develop the necessary Spiritual Tools to govern ourselves accordingly in any situation, circumstance, or event, especially when we are experiencing some sort of upset, distraction, provocation, or testing.

The Spiritual Tools needed will vary from person to person, situation to situation, blueprint to blueprint, trauma to trauma, and so on. So, it behooves us to involve the Holy Trinity in all things. It helps us cover all of our Spiritual Bases, *As It Pleases God*. Doing so assists us in connecting to the Kingdom of God, *Spirit to Spirit*, as well as our Spiritual Covering through the Blood of Jesus. Plus, if we are in Purpose on purpose or actively using our Gifts, Calling, Talents, or Creativity, they will create the Spiritual Polish for our daily ventures.

From the Ancient of Days until now, the precious commodities of *Love, Joy,* and *Happiness* will avail themselves to everyone, whether we understand them or not. The Cycle of Life and the Heavenly of Heavens are not biased. It is an equal opportunity force to be reckoned with, revealing the Cycles of *Love, Joy,* and *Happiness* in all things. When we begin to pay attention, mainly to the small things we take for granted, we will see what is in plain sight.

When life offers its precious and most valued commodities in our Earthen Vessels, showing us the way to the richness of living life with a Heaven on Earth Experience, if we reject it, we become internally weak. How is this possible? It is due to the natural elements or forces of the Great Unknown wrapped in the components hidden in our connection to gratitude. Science has yet to figure out the true dynamics of gratefulness, but it is so real beyond what we could imagine.

As a Word to the Wise, if one has ever felt as if life is pouncing upon them with little or no mercy, it is always best to check the level or Seeds of ungratefulness. Amazingly, it saves a lot of time and heartache. According to the Heavenly of Heavens, ungratefulness is attached to negativity, confounding the wise from time to time. For this reason, it is in our best interest to become extremely cautious, giving thanks in everything, regardless of how it appears to the naked eye.

When dealing with a Kingdom Mentality or operating with Kingdom Credentials, all things work together for our good. Thus, we are required to look for a win-win and the *Courage* needed to move forward in the Spirit of Excellence. Everything is NOT as it appears. There is a hidden lesson, testing, Blessing, benefit, knowledge, Divine Wisdom, or something attached that we should not overlook. Plus, it is our responsibility to Spiritually Dissect the questionables or the brow-raisers.

Unbeknown to most, if we consistently resist what is good, we attract the bad by default due to the *Gravitational Pull* within the human psyche or our Bloodline, regardless of whether we understand it or not. What if we look for the good and cannot find it? First, we need to document our findings, lessons, questions, doubts, or whatever. Secondly, we must understand that there will always be a positive perspective. We simply need to reverse the negative into a positive through our ability to recognize or become aware of it. And thirdly, give thanks, do not dwell, and keep it moving.

Objectively speaking, there are times when the knowledge of the win-win will come later; however, it is our responsibility to develop a Spiritual Journal or Mind Map to capture the win-win in writing as a form of positive Kingdomly Reflection.

When we master the Art of *Love, Joy,* and *Happiness, As It Pleases God*, we will find peace will begin to abide if we allow it to do so. What does this mean? Without the ability to *Love*, experience *Joy*, or embrace *Happiness*, we cannot truly experience peace from the inside out the way God intended, nor will *Courage* reside from within. It is for this reason that we find ourselves playing pretend. Pretending to Love. Pretending to be Joyful. Pretending to be Happy. And most of all, pretending to be at Peace.

According to the Heavenly of Heavens, we do not need anyone outside of ourselves to experience this ultimate bliss of *Love, Joy,* and *Happiness*. All we need to do is manifest the positive energy within our ability to love God, ourselves, and others. Then, the *Gravitational Pull* of our Heaven on Earth Experience jumpstarts our Spiritual Cycle. Whereas if we exhibit hate, it does the opposite, shutting down our Spiritual Cycle, converting it into a worldly tailspin instead. How do we know the difference? The *Gravitational Pull* is determined by our fruits, as well as the Seeds sown in or out of season, creating positive or negative opportunities in all areas.

The goal is NOT to develop an addictive or controlling demeanor when engaging in the Art of *Love, Joy,* and *Happiness*. It makes us desperate, a victim or a victimizer, while outright zapping our peace. If this is not uprooted or rectified accordingly, we will find ourselves becoming our worst enemy from the inside out. How is this possible? It contributes to negative charactorial behaviors associated with us fighting against ourselves, turning on others, or weaponizing what God has designed to liberate us.

The bottom line is that *Love, Joy,* and *Happiness* remind us of the beauty of life and the goodness of humanity. May we always strive to spread *love, joy,* and *happiness* wherever we go. And let us never forget to cherish our precious moments as we bask in the warmth of the Divine Illumination they provide, *As It Pleases God*.

Chapter Four

WEAPONS OF HOPE

The Spiritual War that ensued for our Heaven on Earth Experience is real beyond anything we could ever imagine. Now, what is more real is what we do not often talk about, and that is our fight for *Hope* and *Courage* to face another day. In all reality, this Spiritual Battle supersedes whatever we can see in plain sight, whatever we may perhaps hear audibly, or what we can antiquatedly speak with our outside voice, making the possible seemingly impossible.

All in all, according to the Heavenly of Heavens, for the sake of our *Weapons of Hope*, we must gain the *Courage* to look from within with our Spiritual Eye, hear the unheard with our Spiritual Ear, and speak with our inside voice the Language of the Kingdom, *As It Pleases God*. Although this is not difficult to do, if we do not KNOW what to do or HOW, then it becomes very challenging, making our roar become a subtle purr or turning our vision into a blur.

We all know Hebrews 11:1 says, "*Faith is the substance of things hoped for, the evidence of things not seen.*" But we must also take this a step further; along with our FAITH, we need two additional items to safeguard and spearhead our *Weapons of Hope*.

As It Pleases God®: Book Series

First, we need our unseen Spiritual Weapons to clear the path of all the distractive efforts or obstacles causing us to retreat from the Kingdom or our Divine Purpose. Unfortunately, the enemy will use fear, lack, and shame to stifle us; however, if we have the *Courage* to move forward in the Spirit of Excellence, we can break the chokehold tied to ruining our credibility and sustainability.

Secondly, we need our *Testimony of Transparency* to contend with the wiles of the enemy, ensuring our Spiritual Gifts, Calling, Talents, and Creativity outlive us. Plus, we do not want to give the enemy leverage in using our past against us, especially when developing our *Courage: As It Pleases God*.

In addition, when we are overcome with the power of our testimony, it ensures we do not succumb to debilitating shame or become *Hypocritical Pharisees* behind closed doors. Nonetheless, if for some reason this happens to us, if we are not prepared, *As It Pleases God*, it will cause us to drop our Spiritual Weapons, especially when we are in a battle or at war with ourselves. Therefore, we must prevent this from happening by proactively working on our *Weapons of Hope* and *Courage* without pretending as if we are exempt from Spiritual Warfare.

Meanwhile, we must also know that the Covenantal Agreement from the Heavenly of Heavens used in conjunction with the *Whole Armor of God* is designed to work on our behalf, initiating Kingdom Advancement. Yet, if we do not gain the *Courage* to Spiritually Enforce it or place a demand on it, *As It Pleases God*, it will remain in our DNA archive.

According to the Heavenly of Heavens, to decrypt our DNA archive, we must develop a powerful *Spirit to Spirit* Relationship with our Heavenly Father, awaken our Spirit to become ONE with the Holy Spirit, cover ourselves with the Blood of Jesus, use the Fruits of the Spirit, and behave Christlike. If we choose NOT to use this approach, we can become a Believer without Divine Access to the Kingdom with a crypt from within.

Clearly, building crypts is not the reason for reading *Courage: As It Pleases God*, so let us break the ice on the hidden secrets of the psyche. If we desire the Secrets and Wisdom of the Kingdom, it behooves us to engage in igniting the *Weapons of Hope* from within. What does breaking the ice have to do with our *Weapons of Hope*? It helps us become relationally involved, equipping us to avoid one-sided selfish relations, behaviors, or conversations.

If we do not develop our people skills, our relational skills, and our boundaries positively, we will suffer negatively. If we do not know how to talk to people or if we are out of control, we will rub them the wrong way. In the simplest way to explain this, we may disrespect them without knowing why, or we may symbolically assassinate them, while appearing right in our own eyes.

On the contrary, while we think we are right, the Kingdom frowns upon our behaviors, especially when we have not taken the time to regraft our fruits positively. Is this Biblical? Here is what it says, "*For by it the elders obtained a good testimony. By faith we understand that the worlds were framed by the word of God, so that the things which are seen were not made of things which are visible. By faith Abel offered to God a more excellent sacrifice than Cain, through which he obtained witness that he was righteous, God testifying of his gifts; and through it he being dead still speaks.*" Hebrews 11:2-4.

Our *Weapons of Hope* helps us regraft our Mind, Body, Soul, and Spirit from worldly to Kingdom. In addition, it assists in breathing life into our Fruits of the Spirit and Christlike Character as well. Why do we need to regraft ourselves positively? Our Blessings are attached to our fruits, but we must uproot the negativity, biases, envy, jealousy, pride, coveting, and unforgiveness, getting rid of the unfruitful or rotten baggage.

What is the reason for getting rid of spoiled goods? It is for our Spiritual Survival and the development of our *Courage: As It Pleases God*. However, before we move on, allow me to align this accordingly: "*Blessed is the man who trusts in the LORD, and whose hope is the LORD. For he shall be like a tree planted by the waters, which spreads out its roots by the river, and will not fear when heat comes; but its leaf will be green, and will not be anxious in the year of drought, nor will cease from yielding fruit."* Jeremiah 17:7-8.

What do we do when the Vicissitudes of Life are pressing us to the point where we want to throw in the towel, giving up people, places, and things we have worked so hard to obtain? Better yet, what do we do when we are in a pit, and praying seems to fail us, our hope is getting bleak, people are sucking the life out of us, God has seemingly developed a deaf ear, and we are ready to explode if one more negative thing happens? In this state, if one needs counseling, get it!

Yet, above all, we need the presence of the Holy Trinity. When we involve God in the equation of all things, we also gain access to the Holy Spirit for Spiritual Insight, Guidance, and Understanding. We also have the Blood of Jesus as a formal sacrifice to cover us amid Divine Intervention. Is this Biblical? Of course, *"Then I heard a loud voice saying in Heaven, 'Now salvation, and strength, and the Kingdom of our God, and the power of His Christ have come, for the accuser of our brethren, who accused them before our God day and night, has been cast down. And they overcame him by the Blood of the Lamb and by the Word of their Testimony, and they did not love their lives to the death."* Revelation 12:10-11.

If we neglect this Kingdom Formality, we will find ourselves fixing or focusing on the wrong things or getting caught up in secret or open distractions. For example, we have a couple fighting over who did not take out the trash. When, in all actuality, one person is mad about being neglected, while the other person is upset about the other person coming home late. As a result, they use the trash to vent their frustrations about each other, omitting the actual reasons for the causation. As a result, it affects their people skills or communicable efforts, eventually breaking down the relationship.

Why would the hidden frustrations affect them? First, they are not honest about what they are really feeling. Secondly, the masks they are putting on are failing them because they are exhibiting negative behaviors. Thirdly, they are not honest about their expectations, which will eventually result in unmet needs. As we all know, unmet needs will cause us to lose *Hope* or lack the *Courage* to continue. Or, it may even cause our *Weapons of Hope* to become dull, especially if we do not recognize the roots associated with our thoughts, words, desires, actions, reactions, and choices.

Amid all things, we need to get to the Spiritual Roots and deal with the Spiritual Fruits associated with 'What' we are going through and 'Why' we are in this Mental, Physical, or Emotional space. Here are a few things that will help us break any negative zone within the human psyche, but not limited to such:

- ☐ We must invest in a Spiritual Journal to *Document* our progress. If not, we will tend to forget the small efforts of progression.
- ☐ We must be willing to *Allocate* time alone to speak with God, *Spirit to Spirit*.
- ☐ We must be willing to *Awaken* our Spirit to become ONE with the Holy Spirit.
- ☐ We must be willing to *Accept* the Blood of Jesus as our formal Sacrifice.
- ☐ We must be willing to take *Responsibility* for our truth, stop lying to ourselves, and stop making excuses for where we are.
- ☐ We must be willing to *Repent* of all of our known or unknown iniquities.
- ☐ We must be willing to *Pray* and *Fast* on occasion, putting our flesh under the subjection of the Holy Spirit.
- ☐ We must be willing to *Cancel* all forms of negative chatter or confusion. While simultaneously replacing it with positive affirmations and Biblical Scriptures to counteract.

- ☐ We must be willing to *Listen, Learn, Understand, Change, Grow, Transform,* and become *Disciplined* once placed in a Spiritual Classroom.
- ☐ We must be willing to *Respect* God, ourselves, and others.
- ☐ We must be willing to *Overcome* all obstacles and setbacks to create a win-win.
- ☐ We must be willing to *Reach Back* to share and help others on their unique journey.

By far, this is not an overnight process; however, it is a doable one, from the beginners in the Spiritual Milking stages to the Spiritual Elites who are on Spiritual Meat.

In a Covenantal Agreement from the Heavenly of Heavens, the Holy Spirit will meet us where we are, with whatever we have going on, but we must be ready. If not, we can yoke ourselves, getting tied up from the inside out. When we play with God, He will become jealous regarding what or who is taking precedence over Him.

Can God become jealous? Of course, He will! We are His Divine Creation; therefore, He has a right to become jealous, especially when we engage in idolatry. However, He will not violate our will, but here is what we need to know: *"I am the LORD your God, who brought you out of the land of Egypt, out of the house of bondage. You shall have no other gods before Me. You shall not make for yourself a carved image—any likeness of anything that is in heaven above, or that is in the earth beneath, or that is in the water under the earth; you shall not bow down to them nor serve them. For I, the LORD your God, am a jealous God, visiting the iniquity of the fathers upon the children to the third and fourth generations of those who hate Me, but showing mercy to thousands, to those who love Me and keep My commandments."* Exodus 20:2-6. Some would say this does not apply to us; whereas, I would say this:

- ☐ We will all have an *Egypt* (A place of bondage) in our lives, enslaved in a Spiritual Classroom, teaching us how to use the invaluable tools we already possess from within.

- ☐ We will all have a *Pharaoh* trying to possess, control, or yoke us to the point where we must make a conscious decision to break the grip, Mentally, Physically, Emotionally, and Spiritually, of the idolatrous efforts.

- ☐ We will all have some form of *Red Sea Experience*. Frankly, this is where we must become delivered or divided from something or someone. Or, it may incorporate severing the ties of our past, allowing us to embrace God's Divine Covenant or Blueprint.

- ☐ We will all have our *Desert Experience*, wandering around in circles, going to and fro, waiting on Divine Intervention. From experience, this is usually where God gets our Egypt (generational curses) out of us as His Love and Mercy prevail on our behalf.

- ☐ We will all have a *Moses* as a mentor hidden in the Thickets, on the Mount, or in the Valley, where it is our responsibility to seek Divine Revelation accordingly. In addition, we must also avail ourselves to the Divine Commandments from the Heavenly of Heavens, which are already written on the Spiritual Tablet of everyone's heart.

Once we are faced with or have endured the traumas of our Egypt, we cannot allow it to bankrupt or corrupt us to the core. We must use the Fruits of the Spirit to survive and Christlike Character as our *Weapon of Hope*.

How is it possible to behave in a Christlike manner when life is throwing blows at us, taking its best shot? From experience, this is the prime time to turn up the volume on the Godly material we are made of. It is only a TEST, symbolically training us in the *Weapons of Hope*. Am I pulling for straws? Absolutely not. According to Revelation 2:10, it says, *"Do not fear any of those things which you are about to suffer. Indeed, the devil is about to throw some of you into prison, that you may be tested, and you will have tribulation ten days. Be faithful until death, and I will give you the Crown of Life."*

What are some of the *Spiritual Weapons* associated with our Kingdomly Crown? Listed below are a few, but not limited to such:

- ☐ The Weapon of Confidence.
- ☐ The Weapon of Expectation.
- ☐ The Weapon of Optimism.
- ☐ The Weapon of Anticipation.
- ☐ The Weapon of Courage.
- ☐ The Weapon of Hopefulness.
- ☐ The Weapon of Faith.
- ☐ The Weapon of Cheerfulness.
- ☐ The Weapon of Positivity.
- ☐ The Weapon of Happiness.
- ☐ The Weapon of Peacefulness.
- ☐ The Weapon of Lovability.

Why do we need to know about our *Spiritual Weapons of Hope*? According to scripture, *"The heart is deceitful above all things, and desperately wicked; who can know it? I, the LORD, search the heart, I test the mind, even to give every man according to his ways, according to the fruit of his doings."* Jeremiah 17:9-10.

From my perspective, a *Q and A Session* works very well in pinpointing our motives, thoughts, desires, and so on. More importantly, it helps us open our Spiritual Eyes, Ears, and Mouth to engage in a *Spirit to Spirit* conversation with the Heavenly of Heavens. Really? Yes, really! Revelation 2:11 tells us, "*He who has an ear, let him hear what the Spirit says to the churches. He who overcomes shall not be hurt by the second death.*"

When faced with any form of crisis, if we question ourselves amid what we are going through, it will force our psyche to answer us or reveal our motives. How do we use the *Spiritual Weapons* in a *Q and A Session* with ourselves? For example, but not limited to this form of questioning:

- ☐ Am I exhibiting *Confidence* in this matter?
- ☐ Are my *Expectations* valid, reasonable, or according to Kingdom Standards?
- ☐ Am I *Optimistic* amid what I am enduring?
- ☐ Am I *Anticipating* a win-win or positive outcome?
- ☐ Am I exhibiting a *Courageous* attitude, behaviors, or proactiveness?
- ☐ Am I *Hopeful* about the outcome?
- ☐ Am I living by *Faith* and not by sight?
- ☐ Am I *Cheerful* regardless of what I see with my naked eyes?
- ☐ Am I focused on the *Positive*, casting down all forms of negativity or defeat?
- ☐ Am I embracing the outer experiences of *Happiness*, giving thanks in all things?
- ☐ Am I manifesting a *Peaceful* state of being from the inside out?
- ☐ Am I exhibiting the Spirit of *Love* in all things, along with the other Fruits of the Spirit?

When asking questions, we must make sure we document our responses, whether good, bad, or indifferent. Why should we document? In my opinion, it is a Divine Form of Spiritual RESPECT. Frankly, if I had not documented, *As It Pleased God*, you would not be reading this book right now!

In my Divine Walk, regardless of what anyone says about me, one thing I do know is that the Voice of God is real, living, and on point. Thus, He will speak to anyone who avails themselves to listen, learn, grow, and sow back into the Kingdom without becoming selfishly pompous. Once again, here is the Divine Decree: "*He who has ears to hear, let him hear!*" Matthew 13:9.

Besides, what is the purpose of receiving answers from the Holy of Holies if we fail to document them, especially when we cannot remember the answers or they fall among the thorns? To be clear, I am not saying we all have a bad memory; however, the Vicissitudes of Life can become atrocious, choking the life out of our Seeds or answers.

According to scripture, "*Then He spoke many things to them in parables, saying: 'Behold, a sower went out to sow. And as he sowed, some seed fell by the wayside; and the birds came and devoured them. Some fell on stony places, where they did not have much earth; and they immediately sprang up because they had no depth of earth. But when the sun was up they were scorched, and because they had no root they withered away. And some fell among thorns, and the thorns sprang up and choked them. But others fell on good ground and yielded a crop: some a hundredfold, some sixty, some thirty.*" Matthew 13:3-8.

Where is the good ground? It will vary from person to person, but I will say that good note-taking will assist us in pinpointing the grounds of the good, bad, and ugly!

On the other hand, if we desire our Spiritual Crops to yield, we must take care of and nurture our Seeds of Wisdom, Grace, and Mercy. What does this mean? We must spend time with them to ensure proper growth, preventing harmful weeds from growing up, choking the life out of our Spiritual Harvest, or distracting us from Spiritually Tilling the ground.

When we are at our worst, or it appears as if nothing is happening, we must continue to do the right thing when wrong things are happening. For sure, even if we do not visually see the fruits of our positive labors, they still hold the goodness inside. Plus, doing the right thing gives us Spiritual Leverage, especially when using *Spiritual Weapons*. But more importantly, if we do these few things, they will give us *Spiritual Brownie Points* or put *Icing on the Cake*, but not limited to such:

- ☐ Keep a smile on our face amid all. We must become joyful from within, regardless of how it appears to the naked eye.

- ☐ Treat people kindly, especially when they are treating us like a junkyard dog or are rude to us.

- ☐ Exhibit wholehearted respect to everyone, even when disrespected, neglected, abused, or misused.

- ☐ Love others with no strings attached, removing the judgmental conditions.

- ☐ Exhibit peace in all things, looking for ways to maintain positive harmony.

- ☐ Proactively help or share with others in our time of need or theirs.

- ☐ Become patient with God, ourselves, and others, extending mercy and compassion.

- ☐ Pray and worship God amid the Vicissitudes of Life, remembering God is on the Throne.

- ☐ Learn how to communicate effectively, speaking or sharing information without offending or becoming angry, rude, demeaning, judgmental, or aggressive.

- ☐ Do not become afraid to go into the mud to draw someone out who desperately cries out for help. In addition, it is vital to assist without drawing attention to it or making the recipient feel obligated or indebted.

- ☐ Be GRATEFUL while becoming a good steward over what we have, without fantasizing about the grass being greener on the other side.

- ☐ Refuse to support or justify negativity or bad behavior, especially when Spiritual Blindness, Deafness, or Muteness is involved. If we have been enlightened, we do not want darkness to cloud our sense of good judgment, spoil our fruits, or taint our character; therefore, we must deflect it with positivity and righteousness, period!

Once the training is over, God will open the Windows of Heaven and pour out a Blessing we will not have enough room to store. How is this possible? Allow me to answer this question with scripture, *"And the disciples came and said to Him, 'Why do You speak to them in parables?' He answered and said to them, 'Because it has been given to you to know the Mysteries of the Kingdom of Heaven, but to them it has not been given.' For whoever has, to him more will be given, and he will have abundance; but whoever does not have, even what he has will be taken away from him."* Matthew 13:10-12.

According to the Heavenly of Heavens, our *Hope* is what keeps our Spiritual Faith and *Courage* alive. The little ray of *Hope* may not appear as much to others, but it will give our mustard seed Faith the illumination it needs to grow COURAGEOUSLY, especially if we do not give up or give in.

As the sun rises in the east and sets in the west, keep in mind that every day gives us new opportunities to embrace a Greater Hope residing within. How do we make this make sense? Our greatest *Weapon of Hope* is Love. According to Romans 13:10, here is what we must know: *"Love does no harm to a neighbor; therefore, love is the fulfillment of the law."* When we begin to approach life in such a manner, it changes the trajectories within the human psyche by default. How is this possible? Everything we do, say, feel, or become is associated with some form of love or its lack.

Suppose we have an issue with anything or anyone having nothing to do with ungratefulness. In this case, it is always best to pinpoint the love or lack factor, bridging the solutions outwardly. If we do not get to the love root or its lack, our negative fruits dealing with selfishness will remain with varying characters, depending on what or who we are dealing with. Then again, it could predicate itself on what is dealing with us. Unfortunately, it will follow us like a shadow, appearing when the right amount of light reflects at the slight angle of our issue, weakness, kryptonite, habit, and so on.

So, if we choose to Mind Map the love or lack of love factors associated with our regrafting process, I would consider this a smart move. It helps us to heal and not just develop a temporary scab as a form of cover-up. Amid healing on any level, we must be willing to make peace with our past, bearing no grudges. This Optimistic Weapon of approach helps us forgive, let go, and move on. Our past was our training ground, moving us to the next level; therefore, we must focus on elevation instead of the degrading and demoralizing effects associated with unforgiveness or selfishness.

In my opinion, we should say *'Thank You'* to whatever or whomever while learning the lessons needed to avoid any form of repetitiveness and keep it moving. Amid all, the Cycle of Life has no mercy on us if we fail to learn, grow, and sow back into the Kingdom. What about the Mercy of God? According to the Heavenly of Heavens, mercy is available to all and withheld from no one. On the other hand, He also offers Divine Mercy to those making a wholehearted attempt to become or grow into righteousness, *As It Pleases Him*. It is also extended to those who do not use regular mercy as a crutch or an excuse to engage in debauchery, selfishness, disobedience, or satiate soulish lusts.

Therefore, we cannot abuse the Spiritual System because there is a big difference between regular mercy and Divine Mercy.

Spiritually Speaking, we should not want to cry wolf when it comes down to Divine Grace and Mercy. We should reserve this right to call in Spiritual Backup in our real time of need, especially when we know we are dead wrong in the commission of some form of debauchery. For our sake, this also includes mistakes involving the lust of the eyes, the lust of the flesh, or the pride of life.

Unbeknown to most, when we hold on to anger, hatefulness, bitterness, unforgiveness, envy, jealousy, greed, pride, or coveting, we limit the effectiveness of our training, dulling our weaponry. What does this mean? With this condition of the heart, in the Kingdom, we can only go so far. What is the limit on how far we are allowed to go? It will vary from person to person, mission to mission, gift to gift, and so on. However, I will say this: For those of a Higher Calling, a Spiritual Elite, or those on a time-sensitive commission, God will pump the brakes on us so fast that it will make our heads spin. Plus, the Rod of Correction is fierce beyond anything we can ever imagine, especially when the beatdown from the inside out is of our own making. So, it is always best to self-correct before Spiritual Correction takes place or the Wrath of God stops us in our tracks, especially when dealing with the Tree of Life.

Why do we need to know about the *Tree of Life* as it relates to our *Weapon of Hope*? According to the Heavenly of Heavens, "*Hope deferred makes the heart sick, but when the desire comes, it is a Tree of Life.*" Proverbs 13:12. Why do we become sick when our Spiritual Access is denied? The *Tree of Life* is hidden within us, containing our Gifts, Calling, Talents, Purpose, and Creativity, invoking the *Courage* we all seek.

Unbeknown to most, the *Tree of Life* is Spiritually Guarded. Here is the scripture to align, it says, "*So He drove out the man; and He placed cherubim at the east of the garden of Eden, and a flaming sword which turned every way, to guard the way to the Tree of Life."* Genesis 3:24.

What do our fruits or character have to do with why the *Tree of Life* is Spiritually Guarded? It was disobedience that caused this problem in the first place; therefore, it is OBEDIENCE that is going to set the record straight, *As It Pleases God*. Therefore, we are required to do our part in the equation, Spiritually Tilling our own ground, making our fruits righteous and our character more Christlike. Is this Biblical? *"He who troubles his own house will inherit the wind, and the fool will be servant to the wise of heart. The fruit of the righteous is a Tree of Life, and he who wins souls is wise. If the righteous will be recompensed on the earth, how much more the ungodly and the sinner."* Proverbs 11:29-31.

More importantly, when our *Weapons of Hope* or *Courage* come under attack, remember that the *Spiritual Weapons of Warfare* are readily available to use at our beck and call. So, in the next chapter, we will go deeper into an understanding of how to use them without selling ourselves short or losing *Courage*.

Chapter Five

SPIRITUAL WEAPONS

Most of us think our Blessings are just about money or material gain; however, this could not be further from the truth. In seeking answers or the *Courage* to possess our Blessings, *As It Pleases God*, it will come wrapped in the intangibilities from the Heavenly of Heavens, associated with our Divine Blueprint or Birthrights.

Unbeknown to most, the Unseen Elements are guarding the Spiritual Access to our Gifts, Calling, Talents, Purpose, or Creativity. What does this mean? Once again, Spiritual Guards are protecting our Garden of Eden (our Divine Blueprint). One set of Guards is attempting to keep us from obtaining what rightly belongs to us. The other guards are preventing illegal entry to the Promises of God. After all, the Spiritual Guards are similar to good and evil, right and wrong, just and unjust, and so on. They are on their duty post, doing what they are Divinely Commissioned to do, and do not play around.

More importantly, with this Spiritual Access, we must possess what 'Money Cannot Buy.' Now, to do so, we must come to an understanding of what money CAN buy. What is the purpose of knowing this information? If we can buy it, it is not a KEY to the Kingdom! For this reason, God will TEST us thoroughly before we are able to possess the FULL PORTION of our Divine Birthrights or Blueprint.

What do we need to gain this sort of Spiritual Access? We need Self-Control to gain access to the Mysteries, Secrets, and Wisdom of the Kingdom. Is Self-Control a character trait? Of course, it is! In the same way we get out of character, we can exhibit Self-Control as a form of mannerism to align our character or to get back into character according to Kingdom Standards. What does this mean exactly? We must have Self-Control, period.

To combat the downfall of mankind, we must deal with three areas: the lust of the eyes, the lust of the flesh, and the pride of life. To be clear, this does not mean we have perfect control. No one is absolutely perfect, even if they have a great game of pretense going on.

Ideally, according to the Will of the Kingdom, the willful control to become a work-in-progress to self-correct through the vehicle of Forgiveness and Repentance is the ultimate intent. By far, it is one of the best ways to avoid abusing the Spiritual System of Conveyance or Kingdom Privileges.

Furthermore, without Self-Control, we cannot truly master our *Weapons of Hope*, even if we pretend to be experts. Why would this be the case, especially when we have free will to master whatever and with whomever? According to the Heavenly of Heavens, God is still on the Throne, which means Divine Order is still in place regarding our Heaven on Earth Experience. And, regardless of our freedom of agility, the lack of Self-Control dulls our *Spiritual Weapons* while rewarding us with blank ammunition instead.

Listen, according to the Heavenlies, shooting blanks in the Realm of the Spirit is dangerous, especially when it is unjustified. If we attack or target a Spiritual Elite with unjustifiable weaponry of foolery or with a lack of understanding in this area, their Divine Veil of Protection will step in. Once this happens, it will cause our blank shots to ricochet, backfiring as fully loaded ammunition from a Spiritual Perspective.

As a word of extreme caution, when it comes down to the Divine Veil, circumventing the Divine Blueprint of someone who is in Purpose on purpose, an individual who is on their Spiritual Mount, or when we openly contend with the Will of God, we never know where the ammunition will land. What does this mean? For example, this is similar to shooting live rounds of bullets in the air. Once we pull the trigger, setting a bullet in motion, we cannot govern where the *Gravitational Pull* will cause it to land. Meanwhile, the same happens in the Spiritual Realm as well.

When God has Spiritually Anointed something or someone for a specific PURPOSE, whatever it is, it becomes a LIVE WIRE, similar to what happened on Mount Sinai in Exodus 19. However, this is what I want to extract: *"Then the LORD said to Moses, 'Go to the people and consecrate them today and tomorrow, and let them wash their clothes.' And let them be ready for the third day. For on the third day the LORD will come down upon Mount Sinai in the sight of all the people. You shall set bounds for the people all around, saying, 'Take heed to yourselves that you do not go up to the mountain or touch its base.' Whoever touches the mountain shall surely be put to death. Not a hand shall touch him, but he shall surely be stoned or shot with an arrow; whether man or beast, he shall not live.' When the trumpet sounds long, they shall come near the mountain. So Moses went down from the mountain to the people and sanctified the people, and they washed their clothes. And he said to the people, be ready for the third day; do not come near your wives."* Exodus 19:10-15.

To safeguard ourselves and others, we must have Self-Control and Spiritual Insight on full alert, *As It Pleases God*. This stance of reverence ensures we do not tread upon uncharted, reserved, or forbidden territory while becoming careful about 'What' or 'Who' we touch when He is moving.

When undulling our *Spiritual Weapons*, we must exercise Self-Control and do everything in the Spirit of Righteousness regarding 'What' we set in motion, 'How' we go about doing so, 'Where' we are doing it, 'When' we choose to do it, our reasons 'Why,' and with 'Whom.' What makes our approach so important? We do not want any negative darts or ammunition to target our children, household, Bloodline, or us due to some form of selfishness, revenge, or biased reasoning.

How do we know if we are shooting dull, blank ammunition or negative darts? We will become Mentally, Physically, Emotionally, and Spiritually exhausted with self-created issues. Then again, we may lack Spiritual Power with the *'All bark and no bite'* demeanor with zero amounts of *Courage*. But do not take my word for it; let us take it to scripture: *"If the ax is dull, and one does not sharpen the edge, then he must use more strength; but wisdom brings success."* Ecclesiastes 10:10. For this reason, our habits, vices, and lusts really expose our level of Self-Control, gauging our Spiritual Sharpness, Elitism, or Commissionability.

So, as a Word to the Wise, beware of the loudest person in the room! What does this have to do with anything? In the Kingdom, we have Spiritual Protocol, period! Speaking out of turn, vociferously, unpeaceably, abrasively, arrogantly, or overbearingly creates Kingdom Violations, spoiling the Fruits of our Spirit, affecting our Christlike Character, and zapping our *Courage*.

Is it not insulting or degrading to call someone dull or say that someone is shooting blank ammunition? It is not 'What' we say; it is the 'Way' we say it, as well as our reasoning behind 'Why' we are doing so! However, in the Union of Oneness with the Heavenly of Heavens, the dullness of sight, hearing, or understanding is more offensive, causing our *Spiritual Weapons* to become questionable, ineffective, flimsy, and putrefied.

To be clear, I am not here to pass judgment; I am here to bring HEALING. So, allow me to align accordingly. *"And He said, 'Go, and tell this people: Keep on hearing, but do not understand; keep on seeing, but do not perceive.' Make the heart of this people dull, and their ears heavy, and shut their eyes; lest they see with their eyes, and hear with their ears, and understand with their heart, and return and be healed."* Isaiah 6:9-10.

When in such a state, how do we return to God and gain the *Courage* to do so? Here is a list to help, but not limited to such:

- ☐ We must *Repent* of our dullness.

- ☐ We must invoke the Holy Trinity in prayer, asking for Divine Help or Intervention.

- ☐ We must list our dull character traits in our Spiritual Journal.

- ☐ We must list the opposite of the dull character trait next to it.

- ☐ We must find the applicable scriptures associated with whatever is on our list.

- ☐ We must create an affirmation to motivate ourselves daily.

- ☐ We must pride ourselves on looking for and documenting the win-win of our dullness; it keeps us from forgetting what God is doing with and through us.

- ☐ We must give THANKS in all things, especially for the sharpening of our Spiritual Blades.

- ☐ We must be willing to GIVE back, helping others deal with their dullness without calling them names. I have found the soft approach with our Testimony works best without instigating rebellion from another. *"Now faith is the substance of things hoped for, the evidence of things not seen. For by it the elders obtained a Good Testimony."* Hebrews 11:1-2.

- ☐ We must proactively practice using the Fruits of the Spirit with a self-corrective method or checklist. What does this mean? When we mess up or omit using a Spiritual Fruit, we self-correct ourselves amid what we are doing. For example, with love, if we do something unloving, we must reverse it immediately, publicly or privately. It teaches our human psyche to obey the Spiritual Protocols associated with the Fruits of the Spirit! Plus, it helps with our transparency as well.

- ☐ We must consistently work on our character to become Christlike in our approach to all things.

- ☐ We must suit up with the Whole Armor of God without fail, ensuring we will not be hung out to dry by those who attempt to take our kindness as a weakness, sabotage us, or who are outright, selfishly pompous.

To be clear, no one is immune to dullness, regardless of how smart, knowledgeable, or wise we are. Blasphemy, right? Wrong. We are all a work-in-progress. Some people will humbly own their truth. Then again, we have some who will choose to pompously live a lie or put on a show when in the public eye. But behind closed doors, once unmasked, the truth stares us in the face.

Unfortunately, denied truths are where our *Spiritual Weapons* become dull, diluted, and disenfranchised instead of sharp, tenacious, and empowered. Before we move on, allow me to interject scripture, "*Everyone is dull-hearted, without knowledge; every metalsmith is put to shame by an image; for his molded image is falsehood, and there is no breath in them. They are futile, a work of errors; in the time of their punishment they shall perish.*" Jeremiah 10:14-15.

If we dare to set boundaries, Mentally, Physically, Emotionally, and Spiritually, we will find we can shut down people, places, and things contradicting our Divine Blueprint.

What is the purpose of shutting down whatever or whomever? Our *Spiritual Weapons* are designed to help us in many ways, putting our enemies to boot. However, we must be *In the KNOW* about them, *As It Pleases God*, and become willing to exhibit the *Courage* to use them at the drop of a dime to gain our *Second Wind of Faith*.

Chapter Six

SECOND WIND OF FAITH

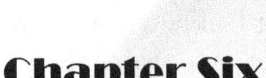

The realization of God being on the Throne helps us put people, places, and things into their proper perspective, giving us the ability to divide, pursue, or conquer based on our *Spirit-to Spirit* Relationship, *As It Pleases Him*. But, most often, the truth of the matter is that what we need most is sometimes what we take for granted the most, due to our lack of awareness, understanding, perception, or conditioning.

For example, we would never understand the value of breathing until we find ourselves gasping for air. The Breath of Life is an invaluable commodity we often take for granted because it does not appear as if we need it right now. In all reality, if we dare to anticipate the effects of not having what we desperately need to sustain life, we will definitely sing a new tune.

To take this a step further, it behooves me to see how we REJECT what or who we need to become better, Mentally, Physically, Emotionally, and Spiritually. At the same time, ACCEPT what or who is detrimental to our human psyche to please ourselves. Do we not have free will of choice? Absolutely! Still, it does not mean we will make the correct choice, *As It*

Pleases God. Thus, the consequences and repercussions are of our own and not of God's, especially when all we have to do is add Him into our equational efforts.

Nevertheless, when grasping for the *Second Wind of Faith*, if we become Spiritually Proactive in our approach to all things, we can better use our Instinctual Nature to maneuver through the vast areas of the Great Unknown, *As It Pleases God*. In essence, in our Earthen Vessel, this is where our Spiritual Covering will help us gravitate to what is suitable for us according to our Predestined Blueprint. While, at the same time, allowing the conscience to become our Spiritual Lighthouse of *Courage*, navigating, flagging, and helping us detach from what or who is NOT according to our Divine Plan.

Here is the deal: We have constructive, destructive, or obstructive proactiveness, which is revealed in our actions, reactions, thoughts, beliefs, spoken words, and so on. However, by taking a moment to anticipate the outcome of whatever we are doing, saying, or becoming, we can make better choices, hopefully avoiding intentional negligence while maximizing our *Second Wind of Faith*.

For the sake of this book, *Courage: As It Pleases God*, our *Second Wind of Faith* is divided into three ways:

- ☐ Worldly Faith.
- ☐ Supernatural Faith.
- ☐ Spiritual Faith.

Unbeknown to most, we have all of them, yet we sometimes fail to understand how they work on our behalf or to our detriment. When it comes down to our worldly faith, it is wrapped in the confidence of knowing that the everyday things in life will work in our favor. Plus, it is also linked to our magnetic beliefs about ourselves and others based on our conditioning, biases, traumas, and thoughts.

From a Spiritual Perspective, our worldly faith is the explainable, natural, or straightforward faith, which takes little or no thought on our behalf. For example, we have faith in how we feel about ourselves. We have faith in our perception. We have faith in our parents to take care of us. We have faith that the sun will rise and set daily. We have faith in our ability to breathe. We have faith in waking up daily. We have faith to know that if we wallow in the mud, we will get dirty, and so on. Why is this called natural or straightforward faith? Usually, these are the things we take for granted while depending upon this ability daily, based on the Law of Causation.

Supernatural Faith, on the other hand, takes more effort, and we have to focus on a specific target, be it positive or negative. Most think Supernatural and Spiritual Faith are the same, but they have totally different uses. What does this mean? We do not have to be in a Spiritual Relationship, go to church, or pray to use the unexplainable elements of our Supernatural Faith for God to intervene on our behalf. Nor do we need it for us to experience a Miracle, defying Natural and Spiritual Laws. Frankly, Supernatural Occurrences are happening all around us in plain sight, but due to our busyness in life, we often do not realize, understand, or relate to the miraculous instances.

By far, this form of Supernatural Faith is like adding a little glue of focused belief to our natural faith, especially when setting goals, Mind Mapping, or being in Purpose on purpose. For example, if we focus on being positive, the *Gravitational Pull* will attract positivity. If we focus on the negative, it will draw likewise, creating events and circumstances aligning with our core. However, if we are ungoverned in using this type of faith, it will eventually backfire, especially when we begin to think we are above God or that we can buy our way through life.

Now, when it comes down to Spiritual Faith, we must deal with Spiritual Laws, Principles, Concepts, Precepts, and Reliance. As a result, we can predict what may happen based on our actions, words, reactions, thoughts, beliefs, biases, and so on. More importantly, to develop our Spiritual Faith, *As It Pleases*

God, we must add the Holy Trinity (The Father, Son, and Holy Spirit) into the equation. If not, we will knowingly or unknowingly cross the line into worshiping other deities for the simulations of what is Heavenly. What does this mean? We will settle for counterfeits, lies, and deception to appear as if we have Supernatural or Spiritual Faith. For this reason, according to the Heavenly of Heavens, we are required to pay attention to the FRUITS. Why? They do not lie!

Respectfully speaking, with big, little, or no faith, we are all a work-in-progress in the Eye of God. Still, when it comes down to our fruits, the difference is whether we are correcting as we go, becoming better, *As It Pleases Him*. Or, if we are self-loathing, becoming outright defiant, bitter, envious, jealous, hateful, covetous, competitive, prideful, selfish, ungrateful, and rude, spoiling the whole bunch to please ourselves.

As the Heavenly of Heavens are opening up on our behalf, there is a little bit of misunderstanding about how our faith is being used interchangeably. What does this mean? If we have a need, we are often told to use our faith, believe, or ask God. Yet, no one tells us HOW! For this reason, we are left to our own devices, approaching faith our way and not according to the Ways of the Kingdom or *As It Pleases Him*.

Whereas we already have faith, we only need to learn how to empower our faith to work on our behalf or disable our negative faith, enabling the positive to prevail. From my perspective, our faith is similar to a light switch, giving us the ability to illuminate the areas of need. While at the same time, powering down the illumination to areas of irrelevance.

Why do we need to power down our faith, especially when we need to be on guard all the time? If all of the light switches are on, it depletes our reservoir prematurely, especially when dealing with issues having nothing to do with us. So, when the enemy attacks us, we are too exhausted to fight back in the Realm of the Spirit. For this reason, when dealing with faith, we must prioritize our dealings to ensure we are not using our faith in areas of deception. The enemy will use distractions relating to our hidden or open traumas, fears, weaknesses, or disabilities to yoke us, Mentally, Physically, Emotionally, or Spiritually, possibly knocking the breath out of us.

When aligning with the Heavenly of Heavens, if we have a desire to become an expert on developing our *Second Wind of Faith*, we must learn how to use all three: Worldly faith, Supernatural Faith, and Spiritual Faith simultaneously. How is this possible? Listed below are a few ways, but not limited to such:

- ☐ We must become *Grateful* and *Respectful* for and in all things. According to the Heavenly of Heavens, disrespectfulness and ungratefulness deplete our power source of inner stability and strength. What is the purpose of knowing this? *"A brother offended is harder to win than a strong city, and contentions are like the bars of a castle."* Proverbs 18:19.

   People will develop a deaf ear to us, especially when we have made them feel less than, we have contributed to their inner trauma, we are a wolf in sheep's clothing, we are never satisfied, we are disrespectfully unapologetic, we speak to them like a junkyard dog, or we are outright unauthentic.

- ☐ We must properly govern what is going on within the human psyche, *Regrafting* it with the Fruits of the Spirit (Love, Joy, Peace, Patience, Kindness, Goodness, Faithfulness, Gentleness, and Self-Control) to develop our Christlike Character. What is the reason for becoming rooted in this manner? *"A man is not established by wickedness, but the root of the righteous cannot be moved."* Proverbs 12:3.

   Our Kingdom Stability from within depends upon our Spiritual Fruits. Without them, we are left to our own devices, having to come back to the *Regrafting Phase* for restoration in due time. In so many words, we can do it now or later, but eventually, this process will occur.

- ☐ We must understand God's expectations based upon His written Word. Why do we need to incorporate the Word of God? *"He who despises the word will be destroyed, but he who fears the commandment will be rewarded. The law of the wise is a fountain of life, to turn one away from the snares of death. Good understanding gains favor, but the way of the unfaithful is hard."* Proverbs 13:13-15.

- ☐ We must *Avoid* the misuse of our faith. Using our faith to engage in ill will causes it to waver. Our conscience will convict us in due time, yoking the human psyche. Here is what we need to know: *"Every prudent man acts with knowledge, but a fool lays open his folly. A wicked messenger falls into trouble, but a faithful ambassador brings health."* Proverbs 13:16-17.

- ☐ We must be *Willing* to listen, learn, grow, follow, and share instructions in or out of the Spiritual Classroom. If we are dead-set on doing things our way, we will find ourselves being the loudest person in the room without any form of Spiritual Power or real *Courage*. *"Whoever loves instruction loves knowledge, but he who hates correction is unwise."* Proverbs 12:1.

- ☐ We must become *Proactive*, paying attention to our natural instincts first and then mastering our Spiritual Instincts. Are they not the same? No one is related to the natural elements, and the other is Spiritual. What does this mean? When tapping into the invisibility of the Spiritual, we must be able to read the Divine Messages sent through visible or natural elements as a form of confirmation.

  However, our *Spirit to Spirit* Communication or Relations will vary from person to person. So, our Spiritual Language must become well-developed, *As It*

As It Pleases God®: Book Series

Pleases God. What is the purpose of developing this form of communication? *"The preparations of the heart belong to man, but the answer of the tongue is from the LORD. All the ways of a man are pure in his own eyes, but the LORD weighs the spirits. Commit your works to the LORD, and your thoughts will be established."* Proverbs 16:1-3.

☐ We must *Pay Attention*, or better yet, we must *Awaken* from our slumber, deflating the negative, unfruitful, unproductive, wayward, and so on. What is the purpose of doing so? *"The soul of a lazy man desires, and has nothing; but the soul of the diligent shall be made rich."* Proverbs 13:4.

Now, to prevent our soulish nature from becoming lazy, we must become a master at diligently working on ourselves on a moment-by-moment basis with a work-in-progress mentality. In addition, we must Spiritually Till our own ground to unveil our Predestined Blueprint. While simultaneously reversing any form of debauchery or hiccups into a favorable, win-win situation, backed by the Word of God and *As It Pleases Him.*

☐ We must remain *Calm* and *Peaceful* amid chaos, confusion, or sabotage, giving us the ability to think on our feet or revamp our approach at the drop of a dime. Why do we need to remain in this manner, especially when it appears as if people are pouncing on us without any form of remorse? First and foremost, we do not have to respond to any and everything.

Secondly, we must know this beyond a shadow of a doubt: *"A wise son heeds his father's instruction, but a scoffer does not listen to rebuke. A man shall eat well by the fruit of his mouth, but the soul of the unfaithful feeds on violence. He who guards his mouth preserves his life, but he who opens wide his lips shall have destruction."* Proverbs 13:1-3.

And, thirdly, *"Better is a dry morsel with quietness, than a house full of feasting with strife."* Proverbs 17:1.

- ☐ We must pride ourselves on being Honestly Transparent without lying to ourselves and others, deceitfully feeding the human psyche. *"There is one who speaks like the piercings of a sword, but the tongue of the wise promotes health. The truthful lip shall be established forever, but a lying tongue is but for a moment. Deceit is in the heart of those who devise evil, but counselors of peace have joy."* Proverbs 12:18-20.

- ☐ We must Trust God, As It Pleases Him. At the same time, we must have faith in the Process or Cycle of Life to prepare us according to our Divine Blueprint while casting down materialism, pridefulness, ungratefulness, and selfishness. *"The backslider in heart will be filled with his own ways, but a good man will be satisfied from above."* Proverbs 14:14.

- ☐ We must focus on Doing, Saying, and Thinking righteously, even when the wrong things are happening all around us. *"A fool's wrath is known at once, but a prudent man covers shame."* Proverbs 12:16.

- ☐ We must engage in Spiritually Tilling our own ground, putting in the work, or doing our part to acquire a Direct Connection back to the Kingdom of Heaven, As It Pleases God. *"He who Tills his land will be satisfied with bread, but he who follows frivolity is devoid of understanding."* Proverbs 12:11.

    What if we are Spiritually Tilling our own ground, and we still are not satisfied with our harvest or results? We need to incorporate prayer to develop relational communication from the Heavenly to the Earthly Realm. It is also important to incorporate fasting on occasion to develop inner discipline and obedience. Why? First, if we cannot control what goes into our mouths, it is also hard to tame what comes out of them as well. Or, better yet, if we cannot control our bodily members, we will have an issue with self-control.

Secondly, praying and fasting will be the only things that could break the yoke of oppression. Is this Biblical? Of course, it says, *"And when He had come into the house, His disciples asked Him privately, 'Why could we not cast it out?' So He said to them, 'This kind can come out by nothing but prayer and fasting.'"* Mark 9:29. Once we master the art of effectively praying and fasting, we need to engage in meditating to still the inner chatterbox, calming the human psyche.

Our time alone with the Holy Trinity gives us the ability to dialogue with the Heavenly of Heavens, *Spirit to Spirit*. Doing so grants us access to *Spiritually Tap In* without tapping out Mentally, Physically, and Emotionally. What if it does not work? First, we must check our Spiritual Fruits and inner chatter. If our *Spirit to Spirit* Relationship is not producing life, it means there is death (a Spiritual Law is Violated) somewhere in our Spiritual Equation; thus, we must check our words, thoughts, and behaviors surrounding our fruits.

Galatians 5:22-23 says, *"But the fruit of the Spirit is love, joy, peace, longsuffering (patience), kindness, goodness, faithfulness, gentleness, self-control. Against such there is no law."* On the other hand, there are Spiritual Laws against *"Idolatry, sorcery, hatred, contentions, jealousies, outbursts of wrath, selfish ambitions, dissensions, heresies, envy, murders, drunkenness, revelries, and the like; of which I tell you beforehand, just as I also told you in time past, that those who practice such things will not inherit the kingdom of God."* Galatians 5:20-21.

Secondly, we must check whether we are forgiving and repenting. Unfortunately, these two characteristics hold more Believers back from experiencing the *Second Wind of Faith* than anything else. It causes us to choke up on doing the right thing or becoming used as a stepping stone or tool, *As It Pleases God*.

As a result of not being a willing stepping stone, we become a hindrance in the Eye of God. Consequently, we unawaringly forfeit becoming a Divine Cornerstone while settling to become chaff in the wind or a footstool for those we step on. Blasphemy, right? Wrong. *"Let them be like chaff before the wind, And let the angel of the Lord chase them."* Psalm 35:5. *"Sit at My right hand, Till I make Your enemies Your footstool."* Psalms 110:1.

So, my question is, 'Do you want to become a stepping stone or a footstool?' Wait, wait, wait, do not answer this question yet...let us go deeper!

Thirdly, we must check our level of gratefulness. Why gratefulness? If we are always in God's face begging, then He will develop a deaf ear to us, especially if we are not listening, learning, and growing, *As It Pleases Him*. It contains underlying layers of something else displeasing to Him.

Ungratefulness causes us to get a side-eye from God, invoking His wrath against us. What if we fall under grace as Believers? With all due respect, grace covers a multitude of sins, but it does not prevent us from acting or behaving like fools! Blasphemy, right? Wrong! *"Although they knew God, they did not glorify Him as God, nor were thankful, but became futile in their thoughts, and their foolish hearts were darkened. Professing to be wise, they became fools."* Romans 1:21-22.

In addition, from God's Divine Perspective, ungratefulness is a sign of a lack of humility, causing us to fail to recognize the GIFTS that have been bestowed upon us. As a result, it will cause a few things to happen, according to 2 Timothy 3:2-5. *"For men will be lovers of themselves, lovers of money, boasters, proud, blasphemers, disobedient to parents, unthankful, unholy, unloving, unforgiving, slanderers, without self-control, brutal, despisers of good, traitors, headstrong, haughty, lovers of pleasure rather than lovers of God, having a form of godliness but denying its power. And from such people turn away!"*

The bottom line is that being grateful is a way of opening oneself up to the Divine Abundance and Grace from the Heavenly of Heavens. On the other hand, ungratefulness closes the door to them, *As It Pleases God*.

And lastly, we must check our self-mirroring. If we are in God's face about everybody else's business without laying our issues on the altar to become better, stronger, and wiser, *As It Pleases Him*, then this could be a RED FLAG! Unfortunately, ignoring red flags and violating our conscience can indeed get the wind knocked out of us. So, it behooves us to embrace our *Second Wind of Faith* as if we are taking our last breath because the Bible says, "*Let everything that has breath praise the Lord.*" Psalm 150:6.

Our *Second Wind of Faith* is at our beck and call, regardless of where we are in life or what we have been through. Here is what the scriptures tell us, "*We give no offense in anything, that our ministry may not be blamed. But in all things we commend ourselves as ministers of God: in much patience, in tribulations, in needs, in distresses, in stripes, in imprisonments, in tumults, in labors, in sleeplessness, in fastings; by purity, by knowledge, by longsuffering, by kindness, by the Holy Spirit, by sincere love, by the word of truth, by the power of God, by the armor of righteousness on the right hand and on the left, by honor and dishonor, by evil report and good report; as deceivers, and yet true; as unknown, and yet well known; as dying, and behold we live; as chastened, and yet not killed; as sorrowful, yet always rejoicing; as poor, yet making many rich; as having nothing, and yet possessing all things.*" 2 Corinthians 6:3-10.

As a *Weapon of Faith*, all we need to do is simply change our Mindset. While at the same time, calling our *Second Wind of Faith* forward, creating the symbolism of the *Tree of Life* from within, spreading outwardly, and deciphering between good and evil while *Standing our Ground*. However, before we move on, let us align this: "*And out of the ground the LORD God made every tree grow that is pleasant to the sight and good for food. The Tree of Life was also in the midst of the garden, and the tree of the knowledge of good and evil.*" Genesis 2:9. "*Then the LORD God said, 'Behold, the man has become like one of Us,* to know good and evil. And now, lest he put out his hand and take also of the Tree of Life, and eat, and live forever'—therefore the LORD God sent him out of the garden of Eden to till the ground from which he was taken." Genesis 3:22-23.

Chapter Seven

STANDING OUR GROUND

The bodacious mark of *Standing Our Ground* can be mistaken as a form of pompousness; however, it is a matter of owning our truth and not being moved by worldly means of deception. The moment we find ourselves running to and fro with our hands on our heads, lacking *Courage* or doubting our next move, it indicates our Spiritual Stance has been shifted. What causes this to happen? Fear and insecurity are the culprits of these feelings. For this reason, we need the Word of God as a form of Spiritual Backup to combat the negative feelings we are all susceptible to.

For some, *Standing Our Ground* can become intimidating, especially if we are new at doing so or we are out of our comfort zone. Yet, this chapter is designed to bridge the gap in this matter, taking us from a wobbly stance to a Spiritual one, geared up with the Whole Armor of God and with *Courage: As It Pleases Him*.

Before we move on, here is a scripture sharing how to *Stand Our Ground*. It says, "Then the king stood by a pillar and made a covenant before the LORD, to follow the LORD and to keep His commandments and His testimonies and His statutes, with all his heart and all his soul, to *perform the words of this covenant that were written in this book. And all the people took a stand for the covenant."* 2 Kings 23:3.

Everything we need will connect or redirect us back to the Word of God without fail. When we are contending with the enemy, standing on a *'wing and a prayer'* will not get it! Especially when we are yoked or in a chokehold, fighting for our Spiritual Right to exist, or needing something money cannot buy. If one has never been in this place, all we need to do is live a little longer, and the Vicissitudes and Cycles of Life will call our name. When it does, we must be ready, willing, and able to contend with the Spiritual Principles, Laws, and Concepts in hand, playing righteously instead of playing dirty, becoming deceptive, or going to the dark side.

What is the purpose of the Vicissitudes? As a part of the Cycle of Life, it is designed to TEST what we are made of, taking out the weak, vulnerable, and naive. Why? The *'Spiritual Survival of the Fittest'* is not something we should take lightly. We are designed to learn, grow, and sow back into the Kingdom. If not, the Vicissitudes and Cycles of Life will come in to prepare us for change from the inside out, especially when we are not getting the hint that our season is changing.

Frankly, it is usually those who make the loudest claims of their righteousness and those who are the most judgmental who are tried the most. Is this fair? Of course, it is fair. Bragging about our level of righteousness is NOT as powerful as the Spiritual Fruits.

Listen, our fruits speak without us having to say one word, put on a show, prove our worthiness, or put on a mask. Unbeknown to most, it takes the same amount of energy to JUST BE righteous, give our best, use the Fruits of the Spirit, exhibit Christlike Character, or humbly repent consistently.

The Kingdom needs Servants, Warriors, and Intercessors. If we possess them all, we are doing well for ourselves. Yet, if we possess none of them, then we have work to do. With all due respect, if we are not willing to serve another, we have issues. If we do not know how to ward off the enemy's attacks or if we play dirty, we have even bigger issues.

More importantly, if we fail to intercede on behalf of another out of righteousness or because it is the right thing to do, this is an automatic indication that our issues are turned inwardly, reflecting outwardly. What is the big deal? It gets into our house by default, especially if we develop a deaf ear or blind eye to the apparent needs of others.

In the Kingdom, it is not just about one person; it is about *us* and *them*! Therefore, we must pride ourselves on developing Christlike Character while possessing the Fruits of the Spirit. It helps us allow the Holy Spirit and the Blood of Jesus to positively work on our behalf, cleansing us on a moment-by-moment basis to build compassionate consistency. Here is the scripture, "*So God, who knows the heart, acknowledged them by giving them the Holy Spirit, just as He did to us, and made no distinction between us and them, purifying their hearts by faith.*" Acts 15:8-9.

In the union of Oneness from the Heavenly of Heavens, regardless of who we are and why, God must use us in Earthen Vessel to reach another. If we are hung up on ourselves, eventually, we will hang ourselves out to dry. What does this mean? We must depend upon another for the same help we refused to share. In my opinion, it is best to proactively share before our need presents itself, ensuring God will meet us at the point of our need.

Listen, the '*me, me, me*' attitude does not work in the Kingdom. We must get our selfish motives out of the way to ensure we are doing whatever we are called to do for the right reasons. However, when we are doing the right things for the wrong reasons, this puts us in the hot seat with God.

How is it possible to be in the hot seat when we are doing the right things? God is more focused on the '*Why*,' more so than the '*What*,' ensuring we do not bring shame to His Name, the Kingdom, or His Whatever. We are not here for ourselves; we are here to make a difference as a Servant, Warrior, and Intercessor, period!

We often think it is beneath us to be a Servant in the Kingdom, whereas it is a Revered State in the Eye of God. Yet, due to this slight misunderstanding, most prefer to become a Warrior or Intercessor without being a Servant. How is this possible when we are Devout Believers? We want the title, but we often do not want to put in the work required to become Spiritually Effective and Powerful on behalf of the Kingdom.

Of course, we all want a life *'Made in the Shade,'* so to speak; however, when *Standing Our Ground*, we must 'Stay on Ready,' casting down our vain imaginations when it comes down to the Kingdom. If not, our Mind, Body, Soul, and Spirit will become the Devil's Playground, where:

- ☐ We cannot serve anyone outside of ourselves.
- ☐ We cannot suit up for Spiritual Warfare.
- ☐ We cannot intercede on behalf of anyone else because we are yoked from the inside out.
- ☐ We have superficial *Courage* to please ourselves, feeding our imposter syndrome.

Are Believers exempt from the Devil's Playground? Absolutely not! He will shoot his shots, and if we are UNPREPARED, it is not his fault for taking the shot. According to scripture, it says, *"Yes, and all who desire to live godly in Christ Jesus will suffer persecution. But evil men and impostors will grow worse and worse, deceiving and being deceived. But you must continue in the things which you have learned and been assured of, knowing from whom you have learned them, and that from childhood you have known the Holy Scriptures, which are able to make you wise for salvation through faith which is in Christ Jesus."* 2 Timothy 3:12-15.

According to the Heavenly of Heavens, we must become a humble Servant first, learning how to *Spiritually Stand Our Ground*, and then standing up for another. For example, but not limited to such:

- [ ] A Servant Mom, Warrior Mom, or Intercessory Mom is a force to be reckoned with, contending with anyone or anything attempting to wreck her home. In my opinion, this is similar to the *Proverbs 31 Woman*, doing what it takes to keep her home intact. While at the same time working on herself from the inside out with strength, resilience, and righteousness.

    To be clear in this matter, as Mothers, we must not bring negative contention into our homes. We must learn how to understand, defuse, address, and deal with whatever or whomever amicably, regardless of the picture society is painting for us. According to scripture, it says, *"Better to dwell in a corner of a housetop, than in a house shared with a contentious woman."* Proverbs 21:9.

    Plus, why would a woman want to tear her home down with her bare hands? *"Therefore, but avoid foolish and ignorant disputes, knowing that they generate strife. And a servant of the Lord must not quarrel but be gentle to all, able to teach, patient, in humility correcting those who are in opposition, if God perhaps will grant them repentance, so that they may know the truth, and that they may come to their senses and escape the snare of the devil, having been taken captive by him to do his will."* 2 Timothy 2:23-26.

- [ ] A Servant Dad, Warrior Dad, or Intercessory Dad knows how to keep the foundation of his house solid while aligning it with Divine Order, Respect, and Provisions. In addition, he is also the discipler according to scripture.

- [ ] A Servant Family, Warrior Family, or Intercessory Family understands the power of teamwork and has each other's back, especially in a moment of crisis. More importantly, they know how to speak the language of

- each household member, catering to their individuality and respecting their differences.

- ☐ A Servant Child, Warrior Child, or Intercessory Child honors their parents and respects others while doing, saying, and becoming better to avoid bringing shame to the family's name. Here is the Covenantal Decree, *"Honor your father and your mother, as the LORD your God has commanded you, that your days may be long, and that it may be well with you in the land which the LORD your God is giving you."* Deuteronomy 5:16.

- ☐ A Servant Leader, Warrior Leader, or Intercessory Leader in the Spirit of Excellence knows when to lead, when to follow, when to shut negativity down, how to create a win-win, and when to call upon Divine Intervention.

- ☐ A Servant Worker, Warrior Worker, or Intercessory Worker does what it takes to get the job done, respecting the mission set forth by their employer.

- ☐ A Servant Friend, Warrior Friend, or Intercessory Friend creates lasting, unbreakable bonds, making this type of relationship hard to replace. More importantly, it is what true friends would fight to keep.

- ☐ A Servant Teacher, Warrior Teacher, or Intercessory Teacher shares what they have learned in their personalized Spiritual Classroom, ensuring others can understand, endure, and overcome the Vicissitudes of Life. More importantly, they teach us how to become a teacher as well, keeping the Cycle of Information or Fountain of Wisdom flowing to the next generation, enabling them to become better than the previous one.

As It Pleases God®: Book Series

- [ ] A Servant Doctor, Warrior Doctor, or Intercessory Doctor gets to the root cause of our issues without sugarcoating the symptoms while giving us a new, vibrant, holistic approach to our Earthen Vessel.

- [ ] A Servant Lawyer, Warrior Lawyer, or Intercessory Lawyer stands for justice and righteousness without defiling the Law of the Land or that of the Kingdom.

- [ ] A Servant Preacher, Warrior Preacher, or Intercessory Preacher encompasses all of the above in Earthen Vessel while aligning them according to the Word of God. When leading God's sheep, we must become whatever is needed at the time, and we must be able to transition accordingly to ensure we do not miss the mark. Everyone will not have the same needs, wants, or desires; therefore, we must rely on the Holy Spirit to relay what is needed, and we must be accurate.

What is the purpose of being accurate? Unbeknown to most, we are held accountable, especially when we know better and willfully choose not to do better. Then again, the same applies when we withhold life-saving or life-changing information. The bottom line is that we cannot mislead God's sheep, nor should we become a wolf in sheep's clothing, period.

The Bible has a lot to say about those leading His sheep. *"This is a faithful saying: If a man desires the position of a bishop, he desires a good work. A bishop then must be blameless, the husband of one wife, temperate, soberminded, of good behavior, hospitable, able to teach; not given to wine, not violent, not greedy for money, but gentle, not quarrelsome, not covetous; one who rules his own house well, having his children in submission with all reverence (for if a man does not know how to rule his own house, how will he take care of the church of God?); not a novice, lest being puffed up with pride he fall into the same condemnation as the devil.*

Moreover, he must have a good testimony among those who are outside, lest he fall into reproach and the snare of the devil. Likewise, deacons must be reverent, not double-tongued, not given to much wine, not greedy for money, holding the mystery of the faith with a pure conscience. But let these also first be tested; then let them serve as deacons, being found blameless. Likewise, their wives must be reverent, not slanderers, temperate, faithful in all things. Let deacons be the husbands of one wife, ruling their children and their own houses well. For those who have served well as deacons obtain for themselves a good standing and great boldness in the faith which is in Christ Jesus." 1 Timothy 3:1-13.

☐ A Servant, Warrior, or Intercessor who is Divinely Commissioned from the Kingdom of Heaven does not play around with waywardness, bullies, or unwarranted attacks. They will invoke Divine Assistance from the Heavenly of Heavens at the drop of a dime. More importantly, they will usher in the presence of the Holy Spirit while covering themselves with the Blood of Jesus as a Spiritual Shield of Protection. They understand their Divine Blueprint, following it to the Letter using their Gifts, Calling, Talents, and Creativity to do the Will of God, regardless of what the naysayers are yelping.

What if we do not feel led to become a Servant, Warrior, or Intercessor? We have free will to do whatever we like and when. Truthfully, whether we realize it or not, in the worldly arena, we are serving, fighting, and interceding for something or someone; and most often, this is the root of our yoke, oppression, or downfall.

Listen, based upon the lies we tell ourselves, it will determine how well we can *Stand Our Ground*, especially when the enemy wants recompense for the temporary benefits or treasures appearing real or rendered. What do we do when this happens?

Usually, we run to God for help, not realizing we must help ourselves first.

How do we help ourselves when attempting to *Stand Our Ground*? First, we must pinpoint the root of our issue, determining if it is associated with the lust of the eyes, the lust of the flesh, or the pride of life, and then REPENT. Is this Biblical? Of course, I would have it no other way. *"Nevertheless, the solid foundation of God stands, having this seal: 'The Lord knows those who are His,' and, 'Let everyone who names the name of Christ depart from iniquity.' But in a great house there are not only vessels of gold and silver, but also of wood and clay, some for honor and some for dishonor. Therefore, if anyone cleanses himself from the latter, he will be a vessel for honor, sanctified and useful for the Master, prepared for every good work. Flee also youthful lusts; but pursue righteousness, faith, love, peace with those who call on the Lord out of a pure heart."* 2 Timothy 2:19-22.

Secondly, we must become wholeheartedly willing to change while invoking the Holy Trinity (The Father, Son, and Holy Spirit) for Divine Intervention. Thirdly, we must pray, and a fast may be required on certain occasions, depending upon how deeply rooted the issue is or our level of rebellion. Fourthly, we must find out what the Bible says about our situation while asking fact-finding questions, taking notes, and documenting positive affirmations on how to reverse our negatives to create a win-win.

Why do we need to incorporate the Bible? We do not want to become unprofitable servants. More importantly, according to scripture, the reason is, *"All Scripture is given by inspiration of God, and is profitable for doctrine, for reproof, for correction, for instruction in righteousness, that the man of God may be complete, thoroughly equipped for every good work."* 2 Timothy 3:16-17.

How can *Standing Our Ground* benefit us Spiritually? When we understand how God operates, especially when we are in Purpose on purpose, it will supersede anything we could ever imagine. How do we get an understanding as such? We must master our Heavenly Language, having nothing to do with the Spiritual Tongues.

To be clear, I am not discounting Speaking Tongues. It will come into play at some point; however, for the sake of this chapter, I am establishing the importance of having a Spiritual Relationship built on our *Spirit to Spirit* communicable efforts. What does this mean? When God speaks to us, we must hear Him without opening our mouths to say one word.

What if we cannot hear the Voice of God? We have too much inner chatter going on, we are Spiritually Blind, Deaf, or Mute, we are Spiritually Asleep, or we have not yet established a personal relationship with Him.

In my opinion, the best way to understand the Ways of God is to begin to communicate with Him in total privacy, ask fact-finding questions, and take notes. Does it work? At first, the connection is a little fuzzy. Once we consistently avail ourselves at a designated time and place, developing Spiritual Intimacy, and wholeheartedly working on ourselves, He will begin to open up to us. More importantly, if we objectively document during our time alone with God, we will find the connection becoming clearer with use.

As a Word to the Wise, we will not hear God speak evil, wicked, or debauched lies, causing hurt, harm, or curses with a one-way ticket into the Pit. Instead, He will deal with the truth about our issues, our motives, character, fruits, traumas, and hidden debris within our psyche.

Listen to me, and listen well. When we have been Spiritually Awakened and we are in a Divine Covenant with God, with the Blueprint He has set forth, the Kingdom of Heaven will open on our behalf. When establishing *Courage: As It Pleases God*, no one can stand against us unless they are a part of the Divine Plan.

Furthermore, outside of the Spiritual Classroom and Tests, we are the only ones who can circumvent the Will of God in our lives. Why are we the only ones? We must willfully surrender this power to another through our acts of willful disobedience, negativity, jealousy, envy, pride, coveting, greed, or lasciviousness. When we are in Purpose on purpose, *As It Pleases God*, if we do not give it up, they cannot get it!

How is it humanly possible to *Stand Our Ground*, especially when our enemies are on every corner waiting for us to slip? We need to elevate our consciousness from worldly to Kingdom, then gravitate the connection from the Heavenly of Heavens back to what we call our Heaven on Earth Experience.

I know this sounds a little off-kilter, but our *Courage* is intertwined in it. Please allow me to align this with scripture: "*At my first defense no one stood with me, but all forsook me. May it not be charged against them. But the Lord stood with me and strengthened me, so that the message might be preached fully through me, and that all the Gentiles might hear. Also I was delivered out of the mouth of the lion. And the Lord will deliver me from every evil work and preserve me for His Heavenly Kingdom. To Him be glory forever and ever. Amen!*" 2 Timothy 4:16-18.

With this knowledge, here is the synopsis made simple. We can break the yokes that are keeping us bound by going to God first, *As It Pleases Him*. And then, come back as a Vessel of the Kingdom, helping others to do likewise, activating the Law of Reciprocity.

Nevertheless, when taking a time-out and getting back into the Spiritual Game, our *Courage* in *Standing Our Ground* requires us to clear out the negative cobwebs, especially when they seem to appear out of nowhere. For this reason, we must dig deep into our human psyche to unveil our truths, creating a clean slate of transparency to become a pristine *Yoke Breaker*.

Performing this Spiritual Dust Buster from time to time cultivates Christlike Character, producing impeccable Spiritual Fruits, even in unexpected situations and when the enemy thinks they are going to have the last laugh. Nevertheless, when using *Courage: As It Pleases God*, He has the final say!

www.DrYBur.com

Chapter Eight

YOKE BREAKER

The sense of freedom within the human psyche will break known or unknown yokes and chains if we allow Spiritual Liberation to occur, As It Pleases God. The truth is that yokes drive some because they do not realize or understand what a yoke is or is not. Plus, often enough, we do not realize our countenance has fallen until after the fact. When we have been tied up or oppressed for so long, we adapt to this condition. Then, when we try to break free, we go into a state of rebellion as opposed to peacefully transitioning to the next phase.

Regardless of where we are, what we are going through, or how we got there, all is not lost. The *Courage* needed to set the captives free, Mentally, Physically, Emotionally, and Spiritually, is hidden within the pages of this book. By engaging with an open heart and mind, *As It Pleases God* ensures the parted waters open on our behalf and close behind us once we get to the other side. What makes breaking yokes so essential for us to do? According to scripture, *"Stand fast therefore in the liberty by which Christ has made us free, and do not be entangled again with a yoke of bondage."* Galatians 5:1.

According to the Heavenly of Heavens, we mistake bondage for security and worldly captivity for freedom. Of course, it is nice when someone has our back or we have the 'Ride or Die' partner. However, we must become aware of whether or not the security we are secretly or openly seeking will yoke us to the core or cause our minds to jump the track. Why am I saying this? The divorce rate is over 80% right now, so something in the pot, plate, or cup is not right!

If we take a look at security, it means safety, right? Some would equate their security with financial stability, forgetting about Mental, Physical, Emotional, and Spiritual safety. Why do we overlook this viable source of information? The word security tells us why, yet we overlook it. We are trying to Secure-It! Whatever our 'it' is, this is the reason for our compromise.

Most often, we are focused on 'Securing the Bag' without 'Securing Purpose' first. As a result, we become yoked, tied up, oppressed, or blocked from the inside out, becoming money or power-hungry and consumed by our lusts. At the same time, it appears to have it all together with the naked eye. To add insult to injury, we do not even realize our Spiritual Eye is blocked, preventing us from seeing what is in plain sight, *As It Pleases God*.

Understandably, we all need provisions to sustain life. To be clear about what I am saying, if we desire to unyoke ourselves, we must change our order or method of operation to Divine Order instead. What does this mean? According to Kingdom Principles, if we 'Secure Purpose' first, we will 'Secure the Bag' of Divine Provisions. Unbeknown to most, God will provide a stream for whatever He has ordained for us to do. Is this Biblical? Of course, Abraham marked this place for us in Genesis 22:14, which says, "*And Abraham called the name of the place, The-LORD-Will-Provide; as it is said to this day, In the Mount of the LORD it shall be provided.*"

When in Purpose on purpose, our Divine Purpose, Gifting, Calling, Talents, Creativity, or Blueprint is considered our

As It Pleases God®: Book Series

MOUNT, a symbolic place of our Heaven on Earth connection or Spiritual Elevation. Blasphemy, right? Wrong!

Here is the Divine Decree for meeting Divine Glory in the Realm of the Spirit without seeing the Face of God: "*So the LORD said to Moses, 'I will also do this thing that you have spoken; for you have found grace in My sight, and I know you by name.' And he said, 'Please, show me Your glory.' Then He said, 'I will make all My goodness pass before you, and I will proclaim the name of the LORD before you. I will be gracious to whom I will be gracious, and I will have compassion on whom I will have compassion.' But He said, 'You cannot see My face; for no man shall see Me, and live.' And the LORD said, 'Here is a place by Me, and you shall stand on the rock. So it shall be, while My glory passes by, that I will put you in the cleft of the rock, and will cover you with My hand while I pass by. Then I will take away My hand, and you shall see My back; but My face shall not be seen.*" Exodus 33:17-23.

Everything Divine is always centered on or linked to a Mountain or Mount, letting us know God will come forth when we center ourselves on the Mount of our Divine Blueprint or Purpose. More importantly, it will always have the self-contained *Courage* needed to climb up and down, or for us to remain in the cleft or valley for safety reasons. How can we make our Mount or Mountain make sense? Here are a few examples, but not limited to such:

- ☐ Mount Ararat. Amid establishing newness after the flood, this is the place God chose for the Ark to rest, reestablishing Noah and his family, connecting us back to our Heaven on Earth Experience. Genesis 8:1-5.

- ☐ Mount Moriah. In connecting to the Kingdom, this is the place where Abraham's heart was tested by God, instructing him to go to this place to offer his son as a sacrifice. Yet, in this place of Divine Provision, He provided a Sacrificial Lamb (ram caught in the thickets) instead, rewarding Abraham's obedience. Genesis 22:2.

As It Pleases God®: Book Series

- ☐ Mount Sinai. Amid our adaptive phases of transitional experiences, this is the place where Moses was given the 10 Commandments, setting forth the Heaven on Earth guideline of God's Expectations. Exodus 19 and 20.

- ☐ Mount of Olives. To keep us *In The Know,* this is where Jesus gave us the signs of the end-time unveiling, ensuring we are not deceived by evil devices. Matthew 24:1-9.

- ☐ Mount Zion. By far, this is the City or Cornerstone of God. Once we understand who God is, we can better put our past behind us to assemble ourselves accordingly, moving into the *here and now,* while preparing for the future.

  How do we prepare for our future right now? First, it is done by putting our sinful nature under the subjection of the Holy Spirit. Secondly, we must willfully embrace peace, wholeness, joy, and purity, all in the Spirit of Righteousness in the City or at the Cornerstone of God (The Will of God). When we are freed from self-condemnation, Mentally, Physically, Emotionally, and Spiritually, we will find the Zion of Peace residing within us with open arms of grace and mercy. Hebrews 12:22-25.

- ☐ Mount of Transfiguration. In the regrafting of our lives, this is where the revealing of Jesus encourages us to rise up *Courageously* without fear, yielding to the transformational process by focusing on Him. Matthew 17:1-8.

- ☐ Mount Carmel. In all righteousness with God's chosen elect, this is where He uses Elijah to defeat Baal, a false god. 1 Kings 18:19-40.

- ☐ Sermon on the Mount. For our sake, this is where Jesus gave us the Spiritual Principles or Beatitudes on how to become and remain Blessed, *Break Yokes*, or reform ourselves, *As It Pleases God*. Matthew 5:1-11.

- ☐ Jesus was tempted in the Mountains with worldliness in Matthew 4:8-10, showing us how to cast down temptation. Our *Yoke-Breaking* power begins with self-control, knowing how to deal with the lusts of the flesh, the lusts of the eye, and the pride of life. If not, our lusts taint our perception of our Mounts, causing a deflection to occur, keeping us wishy-washy from within, and then spreading outwardly. Really? Yes, really.

  For example, when someone is trying to convince me that they are the best thing since sliced bread, I pay attention to their level of self-control. It tells me everything I need to know about 'Who' they are, and sometimes it will reveal their 'Why' as well. Is this passing judgment? Absolutely not. I do this for my sake, not theirs; although everyone has the right to their own level of control, it does not mean I should allow them to affect mine.

  For me, this is called AWARENESS. Based on my Spiritual Observations and Instincts, I know what is for me and what is not! If we do not pay attention, we can deplete our *Yoke Breaking* power by fighting avoidable battles, weakening our bottom line.

- ☐ Moveable Mounts. In the movement of anything in life, we must do our due diligence. When dealing with any form of Mount, it is our responsibility to figure out 'What' our Mount is, 'Why' is it our Mount, 'How' can we proactively do our part on the Mount, 'Where' to go to build Spiritual Relations, and 'When' we need to schedule a certain time to develop consistency or work on ourselves, *Spirit to Spirit*.

Then, after doing our part on the Mount or with our Mount, God will provide the Divine Instructions or Blueprint of the *'How To,' 'When To,' 'Who To,' 'Where To,' 'What To,'* and *'Why To,'* guided by the Holy Spirit and the Blood of Jesus as our Formal Sacrifice to Spiritually Cover us.

- ☐ Mount Language. Our Mountain has a Voice; therefore, we must learn how to speak to it. Unbeknown to most, if we approach our Mountain sideways, disrespectfully, or cluelessly, it may Gang Mountain us. What does this mean? Unfortunately, this is where we become blocked from every angle and with all types of mountainous obstacles, unleveling the playing field.

    Regardless of what our Mount is presently doing or not doing, we have the power to break the yokes keeping us bound, especially if our Mountain is approached or spoken to correctly. *"For assuredly, I say to you, whoever says to this mountain, 'Be removed and be cast into the sea,' and does not doubt in his heart, but believes that those things he says will be done, he will have whatever he says. Therefore I say to you, whatever things you ask when you pray, believe that you receive them, and you will have them."* Mark 11:23-24.

- ☐ Document on the Mount. Unbeknown to most, our Testament is in our Mount; therefore, we must learn how to document accordingly, ensuring what we learn during our journey does not die with us. The bottom line is that our Symbolic Mount must live on, leaving our *Yoke Breaking* Legacy.

All in all, before we move on, let us Spiritually Seal this Divine Decree as it relates to documentation taking place on our Mounts. Regardless of how many times we have been on our Mount or how many times we may have to revisit our Mount to get whatever it is right, do it! What is the purpose of Spiritually Sealing our Mount? When in covenant with the Heavenly of Heavens, this ensures we are crystal clear about with 'Whom' we are spending our time alone with.

In addition, it also helps us to understand 'What' God is expecting from us, 'When' He is expecting it to take place, 'Where' He is expecting it to happen, 'Why' He is expecting it, and 'How' the Beneficial Blessings associated with doing so will profit us.

How do we obtain this Spiritual Seal and the Courage needed for our Mounts? Remember, they are self-contained with what we need; however, we must take action, *As It Pleases God*. Listed below are a few items to jumpstart our Spiritual Journey, but not limited to such:

☐ We must divide our documentation. To be clear, we should have two journals, one for Divine Instructions, Mind Mapping, or *Q and A Sessions*, and one for the Documentation of our Divine Blessings and Testimonies. What is the difference? One is for Spiritual Direction, Understanding, Relations, and Development. The other is for the Spiritual Reflection of the human psyche.

Why do we need to reflect? Just in case we forget about our big or small Blessings, if we get distracted along the way with the counterfeits, the moment we begin to second-guess God, or when we become ungrateful for the journey by the false hopes of the '*Leaks and Onions*' of our Egypt, we can do a checkup from the neck up.

Now, before we move on, allow me to align this accordingly: "*And the LORD said to Moses, 'Cut two tablets of* stone like the first ones, and I will write on these tablets the words that were on the first tablets which you broke." Exodus 34:1.

- ☐ We must set time aside in the morning, placing God first to establish Divine Order and Authority. *"So be ready in the morning, and come up in the morning to Mount Sinai, and present yourself to Me there on the top of the mountain."* Exodus 34:2.

- ☐ We must go to our Mount alone. It helps us to become delivered from people and their opinions, clearing the airway to our Direct Connection to the Kingdom. *"And no man shall come up with you, and let no man be seen throughout all the mountain; let neither flocks nor herds feed before that mountain."* Exodus 34:3.

- ☐ We must become disciplined in doing what we were called to do. By far, it also helps to build consistency without becoming distracted by the Vicissitudes of Life. *So he cut two tablets of stone like the first ones. Then Moses rose early in the morning and went up Mount Sinai, as the LORD had commanded him; and he took in his hand the two tablets of stone.* Exodus 34:4.

- ☐ We must expect to have a *Spirit to Spirit* encounter, taking us from the visible into the Invisible Realm of the Spirit. *"Now the LORD descended in the cloud and stood with him there, and proclaimed the name of the LORD."* Exodus 34:5.

- ☐ God will set the expectations of what He will do for and through us if we allow our Earthen Vessels to become used by the Heavenly of Heavens. The *Beneficial Blessings* are indeed worth our time; this is similar to putting the Blood of Jesus on the Doorpost of our homes, lives, or whatever with whomever. *"And the LORD passed before him* and proclaimed, *'The LORD, the LORD God, merciful and gracious, longsuffering, and abounding in goodness and truth, keeping mercy for thousands, forgiving iniquity and transgression and sin, by no means clearing the guilty, visiting the iniquity of the fathers upon the children and the children's children to the third and the fourth generation.'* Exodus 34:6-7.

☐ He also sets the revered standards of what we need to do to obtain and sustain the *Beneficial Blessings* of the Kingdom. *"So Moses made haste and bowed his head toward the earth, and worshiped.* Exodus 34:8.

☐ We must understand our *Repentance* is our point of Spiritual Leverage in the Kingdom; without it, we become lost in the worldly shuffle. For this reason, it is imperative to get rid of the lies we tell ourselves, while owning our truth, especially when on our Spiritual Mount. Transparency about our weaknesses allows them to become our greatest strengths. *"Then he said, 'If now I have found grace in Your sight, O Lord, let my Lord, I pray, go among us, even though we are a stiff-necked people; and pardon our iniquity and our sin, and take us as Your inheritance."* Exodus 34:9.

☐ We must be willing to use our Mount as a Spiritual Mission to do great works. This Covenantal Agreement is paramount in our Kingdomly Commissioning Process. *"And He said: 'Behold, I make a covenant. Before all your people I will do marvels such as have not been done in all the earth, nor in any nation; and all the people among whom you are shall see the work of the LORD. For it is an awesome thing that I will do with you."* Exodus 34:10.

- ☐ We are required to pay attention to 'What' is going on around us, 'Who' we are around, 'Where' we are entertaining, 'How' it is driving us from the inside out, 'When' we must make our move without fear, and 'Why' we are heeding the command. *"Observe what I command you this day. Behold, I am driving out from before you the Amorite and the Canaanite and the Hittite and the Perizzite and the Hivite and the Jebusite."* Exodus 34:11.

- ☐ We must consistently do a checkup from the neck up, ensuring we do not become prey to those who are not in covenant with our Mount. *"Take heed to yourself, lest you make a covenant with the inhabitants of the land where you are going, lest it be a snare in your midst."* Exodus 34:12.

- ☐ When embarking upon our Mount with God, with our Gifts, Calling, Talents, and Creativity in hand, we must eliminate all forms of idolatry. He is clear about the instructions on what NOT to do on our Mount or lie on His Divine Altar.

  The *Spirit to Spirit* Relationship is an invisible UNION. With this form of Divine Connection, we cannot play around with manmade connective images. Why? The Blood of Jesus is our ultimate Sacrifice, and that is it! *"But you shall destroy their altars, break their sacred pillars, and cut down their wooden images (for you shall worship no other god, for the LORD, whose name is Jealous, is a jealous God), lest you make a covenant with the inhabitants of the land, and they play the harlot with their gods and make sacrifice to their gods, and one of them invites you and you eat of his sacrifice, and you take of his daughters for your sons, and his daughters play the harlot with their gods and make your sons play the harlot with their gods. You shall make no molded gods for yourselves."* Exodus 34:13-17.

Is this not the Old Testament? Absolutely! The Spiritual Covenant, the Ancient Wisdom, or our Divine Blueprint of our Mount has not changed; however, we have. How have we changed? We have become diluted, polluted, and suited for self-demise or bloodline obliteration, causing us to become stuck, oppressed, yoked, and defeated from the inside out without having a clue about the Spiritual Implications of doing so.

To add insult to injury, we are often doing this all in the Name of God, with rotten fruits all over the place, behaving like a hellion on wheels, and a track record of destruction of innocent people. Yet, in our own eyes, we appear righteous; whereas, according to the Heavenly of Heavens, we have a one-way ticket to the Abyss with a self-locked yoke based upon our motives and the contents of our hearts.

For this reason, I am required to fast forward the *Spirit to Spirit* Wisdom to what is current for a time such as this, getting us in Purpose on purpose with our Gifts, Calling, Talents, and Creativity in hand. While at the same time, enabling one to become a devout *Yoke Breaker* of self, spreading outwardly.

Once this understanding is established, whether it is our Mountain to climb or our Mount to stand on, *The-LORD-Will-Provide*; but let us take it to scripture, "*And Abraham said, my son, God will provide for Himself the lamb for a burnt offering.*" Genesis 22:8. As we fast forward to now, Jesus is our Sacrificial Lamb, giving us rights to our Mount.

Even if people do not believe in us, we should never give up on ourselves. To develop *Courage: As It Pleases God*, all we need to do is believe and work on ourselves daily to become better, stronger, and wiser. Here is the Divine Decree to stand on: "*Therefore, laying aside all malice, all deceit, hypocrisy, envy, and all evil speaking, as newborn babes, desire the pure milk of the word, that you may grow thereby, if indeed you have tasted that the Lord is gracious. Coming to Him as to a living stone, rejected indeed by men, but chosen by God and precious, you also, as living stones, are being built up a Spiritual House, a Holy Priesthood, to offer up spiritual sacrifices acceptable to God through Jesus Christ."* 1 Peter 2:1-5.

What does *Breaking Yokes* have to do with our Mount? It has everything to do with it; our Spiritual Mount is a *Yoke Breaking* Strategy that most are unfamiliar with. Here is the deal: The enemy will attempt to yoke, soul tie, oppress, or destroy us because of our Gifting, Calling, Talents, Creativity, Anointing, Mission, and so on, by any means necessary.

Our responsibility is to understand the 'Why' behind the yoke because our Divine Blessings are often wrapped in it. If we do not consciously attempt to unwrap, learn, understand, grow, and sow from it, we may miss the mark, causing another yoke to form to weigh our human psyche down further. For this reason, we should never devalue ourselves to fit in, especially when we are designed to stand out and shine bright without having to showboat. If we take a stand for our Mount, knowing all things will work together for our good, we will have fewer Mental, Physical, Emotional, or Spiritual upsets, zapping our Personal Power or *Courage*.

From a Heavenly Perspective, to become an effective *Yoke Breaker* and Mount Builder simultaneously, we must lay claim to our Predestined Blueprint under the Covenantal Guise of the Holy Trinity. Why must it be a guise? Clearly, this is not a worldly guise of pretense. To be specific, this is a Spiritual Guise of Wisdom, allowing us to become Vessels of God for Kingdom use.

Moreover, when we are ONE in the Kingdom, under Divine Covenant, guided by the Holy Spirit and under the Blood of Jesus as if we are not of ourselves, but on a Heavenly Assignment, God will shut down any and all things detouring His Mission, period.

Our Mount is indeed our Cornerstone, giving us Kingdom Leverage and something to work with, work on, work through, or work toward. According to the Heavenly of Heavens, if we dare to embrace this Foundational Principle, we will not be disappointed. Really? Yes, really. So, let us align this accordingly, "*Therefore it is also contained in the Scripture, 'Behold, I lay in Zion a chief cornerstone, elect, precious, and he who believes on Him will by no means be put to shame.' Therefore, to you who believe, He is precious; but to those who are disobedient, 'The stone which the builders rejected has become the chief cornerstone,' and 'A stone of stumbling and a rock of offense.' They stumble, being disobedient to the word, to which they also were appointed.*" 1 Peter 2:6-8.

When we become compassionately transparent, we give ourselves room to grow amid our flaws with a work-in-progress demeanor. Thus, giving us the ability to become a *Yoke Breaker* from within, spreading outwardly. Why do we need to know this? People are quick to point out our flaws or browbeat us, creating an insecure yoke of depreciation. But if we know and work on our habits, weaknesses, conditioning, or traumas without hiding the truth from ourselves, we can squash the elements of shame or humiliation attached. In a sense, it destabilizes the formation of a conscious or unconscious yoke, soul tie, or oppression, causing Spiritual Appreciation instead of depreciation.

The moment we can raise our Mind, Body, and Soul from negative to positive, evil to good, wrong to right, and so on, we give our Spirit the ability to Rise Up to the Spiritual Awakening. Yes, indeed, the Awakening needed to contend with the wiles of the enemy or to *Stand Our Ground* with any growth point.

What does our growth point have to do with our yokes? Our growth point indicates the stability of the root positively or negatively. For example, but not limited to such:

- ☐ Deep-Rooted.
- ☐ Mildly-Rooted.
- ☐ Genetically-Rooted.
- ☐ Surface-Rooted.
- ☐ Seasonally-Rooted.
- ☐ Anchor-Rooted (Generational Curse).
- ☐ Superficially-Rooted.
- ☐ Emotionally-Rooted.

- ☐ Mentally-Rooted.
- ☐ Spiritually-Rooted.
- ☐ Anciently-Rooted.
- ☐ Self-Rooted.

Our ability to stay connected to our Divine Source determines the types of yokes placed or removed, their origin, and their intensity. The moment we disconnect from our Divine Source, we subject ourselves to the 'Anything Goes' maneuvering tactics. How so? In the Kingdom, we have Spiritual Rules, Laws, and Principles dealing with fruits and character. However, when we step outside of our Divine Covering, especially when dealing with worldly means, shadiness, deception, or debauchery, unfortunately, they become the underlying motives that appear genuine to appease the human psyche.

As a Word to the Wise, when *Yoke Breaking*, we must learn how to *Stand Our Ground* with the Word of God in hand, geared up and ready to go with the Full Armor of God, *As It Pleases Him*. At the same time, we must know the Holy Spirit is on full alert and that the Blood of Jesus gives us the right to cast down any deceptive devices.

Unbeknown to most, if we are shaking in our boots, lacking *Courage*, and expecting someone else to do what we can do for ourselves, we subject our Bloodline to the same yokes as well. Really? Yes, really. Furthermore, if we do not put in the work to become an effective *Yoke Breaker*, we deprive others of the Spiritual Benefits available to us all.

How is this possible, especially when we are Devout Believers? With all due respect, regardless of what we believe, if we cannot or choose not to '*Break the Yoke*' of our own demons, we set the breeding ground for a transfer.

Due to the lack of understanding, resistance, negligence, confusion, or pompousness, our Bloodline must deal with what we have chosen not to. Moreover, the cycle will continue until it is understood and broken; if not, it will pass into other Bloodlines, causing cross-contamination. Is this fair? As difficult as it seems, unfortunately, it is indeed the Cycle of Life, taking out the weak, untrained, unequipped, unprepared, and naive.

According to the Heavenly of Heavens, it does not mean our Spiritual Cycle has to go against the norm of our Divine Design. The moment we breathe the Breath of Life, breaking the yoke of our mother's womb, we are overcomers by default! The key to embracing this Right of Passage is to know we are an overcomer and a *Yoke Breaker*, period!

In becoming or transitioning into a *Yoke Breaker* for the second time, from worldly to Heavenly, we have the power to contend with all forms of cross-contamination. By far, this helps in protecting ourselves, our Bloodline, Purpose, Giftings, Calling, Talents, or whatever is associated with us, having the potential to put us asunder. While at the same time giving us the ability to teach or become an example for others to do likewise.

In my opinion, we should not wait to teach our children *Yoke Breaking* Principles. Why? The worldly system is symbolically training our children. If they do not know how to contend, they will become prey or traumatized to the core, accruing layers of damaging debris that will need to be reversed at some point.

How do we formally *Break a Yoke*? It will vary from person to person, situation to situation, yoke to yoke, Bloodline to Bloodline, curse to curse, and so on. However, for starters, listed below is a way to get started, but not limited to such:

- ☐ We must recognize 'What' the yoke is or is not, and 'What' it is causing in our lives or within the human psyche.

- ☐ We must determine 'Why' it is a yoke, 'Why' it is affecting us, and 'Why' we need to do something about it.

- ☐ We must understand 'How' the yoke originated and 'How' it affects us or those around us.

As It Pleases God®: Book Series

- [ ] We must know 'Where' the yoke rears up its negative head and 'Where' it is taking us, Mentally, Physically, Emotionally, or Spiritually.

- [ ] We must indicate 'Who' is involved in the yoke, 'Who' are we affecting or cross-contaminating, and 'Who' we need to forgive. Be it a person, Bloodline, self, or whoever.

- [ ] We must pinpoint 'When' the yoke appears or 'When' it affects us.

- [ ] We must truthfully identify 'How' the yoke became rooted to us and 'How' we will become an overcomer, and 'How' we plan to *Break the Yoke*.

- [ ] We must '*Repent*' of our role or any form of wrongdoing, including unforgiveness, revenge, hatred, or any form of negativity associated with the yoke.

- [ ] We must find out what the Word of God says about our yoke while taking it to God in prayer. Nonetheless, a '*Fast*' may be needed, but ultimately, it is between the individual and God.

- [ ] We must '*Invoke*' the Holy Trinity (The Father, Son, and Holy Spirit) in the matter.

- [ ] We must '*Detach*' ourselves from the yoke, Mentally, Physically, Emotionally, or Spiritually, if possible. How? By breaking the connection, changing the channel, or simply canceling the negativity associated with it when it comes to mind. What does this mean? We cannot entertain it unless we use it to create a win-win or reverse it positively.

☐ We must document, document, document, aligning the lessons we are learning with our reality to become better, not bitter. Why do we need to document? When dealing with a yoke, creating a Spiritual Journal or Mind Map helps guide us when we get off track, distracted, or have a temporary lapse or trigger. More importantly, it helps us become grateful in our growth process, ensuring we are less likely to create yokes in the lives of others out of spitefulness.

Yoke Breaking is a unique experience or process for everyone. For this reason, there is NOT a cookie-cutter way to break every yoke. Therefore, we must dig deep to extract our truth, to avoid having our soulish nature hold on to the lies, deceiving the deceived. What is the big deal? It is accepting and feeding into the lies and deception that create yokes in the first place, invoking instability. If we get rid of the untruths, we will begin to develop inner stability, allowing ourselves to heal without having the scabs of deception forming or breaking open when we bump into our traumas or sore spots.

More importantly, if we involve the Holy Trinity in this process, it helps us bend but not break when the Vicissitudes and Cycles of Life or Spiritual Classrooms avail themselves to train, grow, and correct. In this process, it is okay for people not to like us; however, it is NOT okay for us to dislike ourselves, others, and most of all, God. Here is what the scripture tells us, *"If the world hates you, you know that it hated Me before it hated you. If you were of the world, the world would love its own. Yet because you are not of the world, but I chose you out of the world, therefore the world hates you."* John 15:18-19.

With *Courage: As It Pleases God*, we should not worry about what people think of us. It will get us yoked and out of Purpose, especially if we do not know and understand who we are from the inside out. Here is the deal: According to the Heavenly of Heavens, we must focus on what we think about ourselves, what our inner chatter is feeding back to us, and then align ourselves with the Fruits of the Spirit and Christlike Character as a Representative of the Kingdom. And then repeat this: *"What then shall we say to these things? If God is for us, who can be against us?"* Romans 8:31.

Our Divine Blueprint is already written. And if we are clueless about it, we will find ourselves incorporated into someone else's Blueprint, attempting to nullify our own. By doing so, it forms an inner yoke, creating an imbalance within the human psyche. Therefore, *"Do not be conformed to this world, but be transformed by the renewing of your mind, that you may prove what is that good and acceptable and perfect Will of God."* Romans 12:8.

How can we avoid yoking ourselves in the Will of God? We must involve Divine Intervention in our daily lives while doing our due diligence. What does this mean? We must involve the Holy Spirit to ensure we are not led astray, Mentally, Physically, Emotionally, and Spiritually.

What can the Holy Spirit do for us, especially when we are yoked to the core? According to scripture, it says, *"Likewise the Spirit also helps in our weaknesses. For we do not know what we should pray for as we ought, but the Spirit Himself makes intercession for us with groanings which cannot be uttered. Now He who searches the hearts knows what the mind of the Spirit is, because He makes intercession for the saints according to the Will of God."* Romans 8:26-27.

Once again, the script for our lives is already written, and if we indulge in the wrong thing or our own thing, we will find ourselves outside of the Will of God. Unbeknown to most, even if we find ourselves outside of the camp, it is all a part of the learning and growth process of Spiritual Interdependence; plus, it happens to everyone at some point. Why? God will TEST us to see what we are made of. When we come forth as pure Gold, it gives us Spiritual Leverage in the Kingdom. Is this Biblical? Absolutely, it says, *"But He knows the way that I take; when He has tested me, I shall come forth as gold."* Job 23:10.

More importantly, here is what we need to know, giving us a Spiritual Leg to stand on when attempting to create a win-win or *Breaking a Yoke*. "*And we know that all things work together for good to those who love God, to those who are the called according to His purpose. For whom He foreknew, He also predestined to be conformed to the image of His Son, that He might be the firstborn among many brethren. Moreover whom He predestined, these He also called; whom He called, these He also justified; and whom He justified, these He also glorified.*" Romans 8:28-30. Therefore, when *Breaking Yokes*, our motives must be Spiritually Righteous to shut down wicked plots. Let me pose another question: "*Can the blind lead the blind? Will they not both fall into the ditch?*" Luke 6:39.

If we are indulging in wickedness, attempting to plot the demise of another, it is considered a dark manifestation of manipulative efforts. Eventually, an ultimate shutdown or breakdown will come as a part of the Cycle of Seedtime and Harvest. Let us align this accordingly: "*Every plant which My heavenly Father has not planted will be uprooted. Let them alone. They are blind leaders of the blind. And if the blind leads the blind, both will fall into a ditch.*" Matthew 15:13-14.

Unbeknown to most, our *Yoke Breaking* power comes when we work on ourselves daily to remove the plank from our own eye without pointing the finger at one another. Instead, we set an example for others to follow with our plank-removing abilities, leading the way to the Kingdom, *As It Pleases God*. What does this mean? A true *Yoke Breaker* is an expert *Plank Remover*. But do not take my word for it; let us Biblically align this: "*A disciple is not above his teacher, but everyone who is perfectly trained will be like his teacher. And why do you look at the speck in your brother's eye, but do not perceive the plank in your own eye? Or how can you say to your brother, 'Brother, let me remove the speck that is in your eye,' when you yourself do not see the plank that is in your own eye? Hypocrite! First remove the plank from your own eye, and then you will see clearly to remove the speck that is in your brother's eye.*" Luke 6:40-42.

A yoke of any form is literally a symbolic plank turned inward. How do we make this make sense? Any yoke must be justified in becoming or remaining a yoke unless it is a generational curse. From much experience, if we pinpoint our plank, kryptonite, or vice, most often, we will find the root cause of the yoke. Really? Yes, really!

For example, *"For a good tree does not bear bad fruit, nor does a bad tree bear good fruit."* Luke 6:43. When *Breaking Yokes*, we must also look for the contributing fruits feeding the plank as well. By doing so, we can regraft ourselves or reverse harmful fruits into positive ones, preventing the yoke from reoccurring or reappearing in a more robust or sophisticated form of yoke.

Why do we need to uproot or regraft the fruit feeding the yoke? Frankly, a yoke is Spiritual in nature, and it has feelings, and it does not like being deyoked. Blasphemy, right? Wrong. We have *us* and *them*. In short, this is what the battle or yoke is all about! *"And when there had been much dispute, Peter rose up and said to them: Men and brethren, you know that a good while ago God chose among us, that by my mouth the Gentiles should hear the word of the gospel and believe. So God, who knows the heart, acknowledged them by giving them the Holy Spirit, just as He did to us, and made no distinction between us and them, purifying their hearts by faith. Now therefore, why do you test God by putting a yoke on the neck of the disciples which neither our fathers nor we were able to bear? But we believe that through the grace of the Lord Jesus Christ we shall be saved in the same manner as they."* Acts 15:7-11. For this reason, we must know beyond a shadow of a doubt which side we are on, becoming obedient to the Word and Will of God. It determines our *Yoke Breaking* power and how much Spiritual Authority we possess. And, once again, to keep a yoke from recurring or fighting us back.

Once we *Break a Yoke*, it should remain broken, right? I am not here to determine what yoke stays or which ones will recur; opportunely, this is between the Yoker, the Yokee, and God. Why? God has the exact details and underlying truths. Now, I will say this: Disobedience can invoke the Wrath of God, making us outlandishly paranoid, especially when His mercy and grace saved us from whatever or whomever. Whether it is regular mercy and grace or Divine, it is left up to God to determine if we are Spiritually Worthy, *As It Pleases Him.*

Here is what the Bible has to say about the *Decreed Warning* to the Children of Israel: *"I am the LORD your God, who brought you out of the land of Egypt, that you should not be their slaves; I have broken the bands of your yoke and made you walk upright. But if you do not obey Me, and do not observe all these commandments, and if you despise My statutes, or if your soul abhors My judgments, so that you do not perform all My commandments, but break My covenant, I also will do this to you: I will even appoint terror over you, wasting disease and fever which shall consume the eyes and cause sorrow of heart. And you shall sow your seed in vain, for your enemies shall eat it. I will set My face against you, and you shall be defeated by your enemies. Those who hate you shall reign over you, and you shall flee when no one pursues you. And after all this, if you do not obey Me, then I will punish you seven times more for your sins."* Leviticus 26:13-18.

How does the *Decreed Warning* to the Children of Israel from the Old Testament apply to us? Contrary to what most would think, it is applicable to us, our yoke, our lineage, and our Kingdom Relations. Clearly, I do not wish yokes upon anyone, but I must advise of the signs of a yoke and how they relate to us in this day and age. Listed below are a few types of yokes, but not limited to such by any means:

- ☐ When we are openly or publically humiliated or brought to shame, crushing our ego to the point where it is difficult to find our way back to God. *"I will break the pride of your power; I will make your heavens like iron and your earth like bronze."* Leviticus 26:19.

- ☐ When we become unfruitful, especially when we are putting in the effort, our fruit spoils anyway. As a result, it makes us unfruitful servants both publicly and privately. *"And your strength shall be spent in vain; for your land* shall not yield its produce, nor shall the trees of the land yield their fruit." Leviticus 26:20.

- ☐ Amid things falling apart, we become angrily resistant to God or the Kingdom. Or, when seemingly doing the Will of God, things become increasingly worse. *"Then, if you walk contrary to Me, and are not willing to obey Me, I will bring on you seven times more plagues, according to your sins."* Leviticus 26:21.

- ☐ When we are faced with all types of betrayal, debauchery, confusion, and destruction affecting our bottom line, while our children fall prey to the same generational curse, affecting their future. *"I will also send wild beasts among you, which shall rob you of your children, destroy your livestock, and make you few in number; and your highways shall be desolate."* Leviticus 26:22.

- ☐ We will experience the silence of God. *"And if by these things you are not reformed by Me, but walk contrary to Me, then I also will walk contrary to you, and I will punish you yet seven times for your sins."* Leviticus 26:23-24.

- ☐ When our enemies come out of the woodwork to destroy us, our families, or anything associated with us, God allows it to happen without Spiritual Intervention. *"And I will bring a sword against you that will execute the vengeance of the covenant; when you are gathered together within your cities I will send pestilence among you; and you shall be delivered into the hand of the enemy."* Leviticus 26:25.

- ☐ When we are in a constant state of lack where we never have enough, we are never good enough, and we are never satisfied with anyone or anything. Unfortunately, this is when the Spirit of Ungratefulness has consumed our lives to the point where we cannot see how Blessed we are, especially with the simple things in life. *"When I have cut off your supply of bread, ten women shall bake your bread in one oven, and they shall bring back your bread by weight, and you shall eat and not be satisfied."* Leviticus 26:26.

☐ When we are filled with anger, rage, hatred, rebellion, and unforgiveness with ourselves, others, God, or life. In addition, it is also when we are consumed with so much fear that we begin contemplating giving up, or we feel hopelessly abandoned by people. *"And after all this, if you do not obey Me, but walk contrary to Me, then I also will walk contrary to you in fury; and I, even I, will chastise you seven times for your sins."* Leviticus 26:27-28.

☐ When we begin to turn on our children, dividing ourselves, our families, and the foundation of our homes from the inside out. What is more devastating is that we begin to treat our children like junkyard dogs or outcasts, treating others better than we treat our own. At the same time, we allow our homes to collapse due to constant bickering, fussing, fighting, comparison, favoritism, and nagging. *"You shall eat the flesh of your sons, and you shall eat the flesh of your daughters."* Leviticus 26:29.

☐ When we have no place of solace, we run from pillar to post without any form of inner healing in sight. Consequently, we begin to latch on to idols, worshipping people, places, and things, forgetting that God is the Creator of it all. *"I will destroy your high places, cut down your incense altars, and cast your carcasses on the lifeless forms of your idols; and My soul shall abhor you."* Leviticus 26:30.

☐ When we are experiencing massive chaos all around us, especially in the church, at home, on the job, with the community, and in our government. But most of all, within the human psyche. "*I will lay your cities waste and bring your sanctuaries to desolation, and I will not smell the fragrance of your sweet aromas.*" Leviticus 26:31.

- When everything we do, say, and become revolves around being competitively cut-throat, or we have to become a sell-out to fit in. "*I will bring the land to desolation, and your enemies who dwell in it shall be astonished at it. I will scatter you among the nations and draw out a sword after you; your land shall be desolate and your cities waste.*" Leviticus 26:32-33.

Unbroken yokes give way for negative character traits to reside within the human psyche, causing jealousy, envy, pride, greed, coveting, and competitiveness to RISE UP in due time, even if we have been trained to suppress them. How do we notice unbroken yokes in our character? Listed below are a few examples, but once again, not limited to such:

- If we are power-hungry.
- If we are degradingly pompous.
- If we are thirsty for love.
- If we are jumping over others to make ourselves appear better.
- If we are using people to get what we want.
- If we are outright selfish and paranoid.
- If we hang people out to dry without having a conscience.
- If we are gung-ho about putting down or criticizing others.
- If we become tyrannical when rejected.
- If we are outright rude and disrespectful, especially to our elders.
- If we are always trying to create a pit for others.
- If we are an uncontrollable liar, thief, or dream killer.

Unjustified charactorial behaviors have negative repercussions. Here is what we must know: *"They shall stumble over one another, as it were before a sword, when no one pursues; and you shall have no power to stand before your enemies. You shall perish among the nations, and the land of your enemies shall eat you up."* Leviticus 26:37-38. In contrast, justifiable good character and Christlike Character have positive repercussions, even if we do not see the fruits of our labor instantly.

How can we become a *Yoke Breaker* amid a yoke or be a yoker? First, we must REPENT for this behavior. *"But if they confess their iniquity and the iniquity of their fathers, with their unfaithfulness in which they were unfaithful to Me, and that they also have walked contrary to Me, and that I also have walked contrary to them and have brought them into the land of their enemies; if their uncircumcised hearts are humbled, and they accept their guilt—then I will remember My covenant with Jacob, and My covenant with Isaac and My covenant with Abraham I will remember; I will remember the land."* Leviticus 26:40-42.

Secondly, we must ACCEPT responsibility for the behaviors and RELEASE them to embrace the Statutes of Righteousness. *"The land also shall be left empty by them, and will enjoy its Sabbaths while it lies desolate without them; they will accept their guilt, because they despised My judgments and because their soul abhorred My statutes."* Leviticus 26:43.

Thirdly, we must understand who the Head Chief in charge is, casting down all forms of idolatry. *"Yet for all that, when they are in the land of their enemies, I will not cast them away, nor shall I abhor them, to utterly destroy them and break My covenant with them; for I am the LORD their God."* Leviticus 26:44.

Lastly, we must establish, maintain, and stand on our Spiritual MOUNT without deviation. By doing so, it will re-establish the Covenant of our Forefathers, even if we are clueless about them. Nonetheless, we are not alone; the Holy Trinity will train us with the same hand that trained Moses. Here is the

As It Pleases God®: Book Series

Divine Decree, "*But for their sake I will remember the covenant of their ancestors, whom I brought out of the land of Egypt in the sight of the nations, that I might be their God: I am the LORD. These are the statutes and judgments and laws which the LORD made between Himself and the children of Israel on Mount Sinai by the hand of Moses.*" Leviticus 26:45-46.

For the sake of our *Courage*, we cannot allow our negative charactorial behaviors to override our sense of good judgment, hindering our *Yoke-Breaking* abilities. Nor can we allow our yokes to break us, Mentally, Physically, Emotionally, or Spiritually; therefore, it is always best to learn how to *Play Clean* to protect ourselves, our Bloodline, as well as our Divine Destiny, *As It Pleases God*.

www.DrYBur.com

Chapter Nine

CLEAN PLAYING

In today's time, we have become accustomed to *Playing Dirty* while not realizing we are doing so. Or we downplay our ability to *Play Clean*. Then again, we get those who are downright debauched, attempting to ruin the credibility of another by any means necessary. All in all, regardless of our hidden motives, we will eventually seek the answers for ourselves, especially when our motives become our reality.

Unbeknown to most, our motives move our lives into positioning, positively or negatively. At the same time, mirroring our secret or open echoes from the heart through the vehicle of our spoken words, inaudible actions, and our bodacious reactions. Really? Yes, really! Here is what the Bible says about this: "*Therefore you are inexcusable, O man, whoever you are who judge, for in whatever you judge another you condemn yourself; for you who judge practice the same things. But we know that the judgment of God is according to truth against those who practice such things.*" Romans 2:1-2.

With all due respect, this unveiling is not designed to point the finger at anyone. This chapter aims to help us gain the *Courage* to *Play Clean* with our *Clean Playing* abilities, which are already.

We often think revenge or Playing Dirty is our best option. When, in all actuality, in the Eye of God, the TRUTH is primal. What does this mean? The Ancient Principles of *Clean Playing* are hidden within the human psyche, covered by layers of lies, jealousy, envy, pride, and coveting. Now, in agreeing with the Heavenly of Heavens, regardless of whether we are *Playing Dirty* or someone is *Playing Dirty* with us, there is hope for us all.

As life challenges us with throwing dirt or shading others because of their dirt, we should become mindful about 'What' we are doing and 'Why' we are doing it. What is the purpose of challenging ourselves to become better, especially when attempting or having the power to *Play Dirty*? In the pursuit of living life, we will never know how our abilities to *Play Dirty* will become a snare for us, yoking us to the core when we least expect it.

As I tread lightly with this subject matter, I do not wish ill will upon anyone; therefore, do not take it from me; let us take this one to scripture before going any further. *"For they are a nation void of counsel, nor is there any understanding in them. Oh, that they were wise, that they understood this, that they would consider their latter end! How could one chase a thousand, and two put ten thousand to flight, unless their Rock had sold them, and the LORD had surrendered them? For their rock is not like our Rock, even our enemies themselves being judges. For their vine is of the vine of Sodom and of the fields of Gomorrah; their grapes are grapes of gall, their clusters are bitter. Their wine is the poison of serpents, and the cruel venom of cobras. Is this not laid up in store with Me, Sealed up among My treasures? Vengeance is Mine, and recompense; their foot shall slip in due time; for the day of their calamity is at hand, and the things to come hasten upon them."* Deuteronomy 32:28-35.

According to the Heavenly of Heavens, misunderstanding and pretense are causing our human psyche to *Play Dirty*. By exposing our fruits in such a manner, we put ourselves and our Bloodline at risk of exposure to rottenness and contamination, Mentally, Physically, Emotionally, and Spiritually.

As It Pleases God®: Book Series

Underhanded debauchery has ensnared more people than we care to imagine, especially when digging a ditch for another without *Just Cause*. Or, better yet, when we create a pitfall for another based upon our perception, biases, or sneaky control. More importantly, amid all, if God allows it to unjustifiably penetrate one of His just Vessels who are in Purpose on purpose, it comes with a double-edged sword of Blessings and curses; so, exercise extreme caution when engaging in debauched efforts.

Why do we need to exercise caution when *Playing Dirty*? One person will inadvertently be Blessed, and the other person will become the stepping stone or footstool, with a generational curse attached to their Bloodline. Is this not kind of harsh? When dealing with the rotten fruits of debauchery, it happens all too often due to our lack of understanding.

Here is how God feels about His Chosen Vessels, especially those in Purpose and *Playing Clean*. "He will say: 'Where are their gods, the rock in which they sought refuge?' Who ate the fat of their sacrifices, and drank the wine of their drink offering? Let them rise and help you, and be your refuge. Now see that I, even I, am He, and there is no God besides Me; I kill and I make alive; I wound and I heal; nor is there any who can deliver from My hand. For I raise My hand to heaven, and say, 'As I live forever, if I whet My glittering sword, and My hand takes hold on judgment, I will render vengeance to My enemies, and repay those who hate Me. I will make My arrows drunk with blood, and My sword shall devour flesh, with the blood of the slain and the captives, from the heads of the leaders of the enemy.' Rejoice, O Gentiles, with His people; for He will avenge the blood of His servants, and render vengeance to His adversaries; He will provide atonement for His land and His people." Romans 32:37-43.

When aligning ourselves with the Heavenly of Heavens, regardless of our perception, when playing in any arena, it is best to play with our hands close to our chest while getting the Holy Trinity involved! What does this mean? When attempting to play with the Big Boys or Little Boys, we must play with our Divine Blueprint in hand. It creates consistency with our Gifts, Calling, Talents, Creativity, and Purpose, ensuring we do not have to pretend to be anyone else or play anyone else's hand to achieve our heart's desires.

More importantly, if we play in this manner, it will cause everything, including the enemy's tricks, to work together for our good, *As It Pleases God*. Here is what the Bible has to say: "*And we know that all things work together for good to those who love God, to those who are the called according to His purpose.*" Romans 8:28. "*In Him also we have obtained an inheritance, being predestined according to the purpose of Him who works all things according to the counsel of His will, that we who first trusted in Christ should be to the praise of His glory. In Him you also trusted, after you heard the word of truth, the gospel of your salvation; in whom also, having believed, you were SEALED with the Holy Spirit of promise, who is the guarantee of our inheritance until the redemption of the purchased possession, to the praise of His glory.*" Ephesians 1:11-14.

When playing with the Big Boys or Little Boys, why are the Big Girls or Little Girls not mentioned? With all due respect, I am not biased here; however, the Big Boys or Little Boys is a common cliché among the Spiritual Elites, similar to the partaking of Spiritual Milk as opposed to Spiritual Meat. Nonetheless, with the Ancient Principles of *Clean Playing*, we cannot become sensitive to gender. Why? In the Kingdom, we are all ONE, having our own role to play according to our Divine Blueprint.

Plus, if we become sensitive about gender, we limit ourselves in the Game of Life, especially when the Vicissitudes or the Cycles of Life disregard our gender biases, doing what it is designed to do. How is this possible? God will use anything or anyone to accomplish His Divine Purpose; therefore, if we become caught up in bashing one gender over another, we may miss the mark, period.

Listen, everyone has a role to play, and if we are not doing what we are designed to do, we very well may have to *Play Dirty*. We will have a void or longing from within. If left ungoverned, we will do anything to achieve the superficial illusion of what we perceive as successful in the Eyes of Men instead of the Eye of God. What can *The Ancient Principles of Clean Playing* do for us? It helps us to grow internally, making us stronger and more Spiritually Tenacious to stand tall for the Kingdom of Heaven.

When establishing *Courage: As It Pleases God*, we must understand that life is a GIFT. We should never take it for granted. Why? It is priceless! Embracing this mindset, *As It Pleases Him*, we will eventually find ourselves in some form of overflow, building better relations and helping to avoid negative triggers. In my opinion, this is one way to allow our good to outweigh our bad, creating a counterbalancing system from within.

On the other hand, if we allow our negativity to feed our bad, it will tip our scales toward debauchery while appearing right in our own eyes. What does this mean? We will not recognize our wrongdoings because it has become customary to us, our conscience has become desensitized, or we have become Mentally, Physically, Emotionally, or Spiritually resistant. For this reason, we will find ourselves *Playing Dirty* with our human default mechanisms hidden within the psyche.

Unfortunately, without the proper Spiritual Maintenance, *As It Pleases God*, the psyche will begin taking the lead based upon *What, When, Where, How, Why*, and *Who* is hidden within our psyche, playing possum. What does playing possum have to do with *Playing Dirty*? The heart's hidden secrets will determine how well we *Play Dirty* or *Play Clean*, depending on our level of exposure and honesty with ourselves, without having a third party involved.

What does a go-between have to do with anything? A moderator can sometimes help us, but they can also hinder us based on their exposure and training from a Spiritual Perspective. How? We are Spiritual Beings having a human experience; therefore, our approach must be in alignment with how we were created. If not, we may have recurring trauma, appearing real, based upon unresolved, hidden triggers. What does this mean for those who like having the opinion of another? We are all different. What works for one person may not work for the next, based on our genotype.

Our genetic makeup has everything to do with who we are as individuals, our method of operation, our process of thought, our perception, our generational whatever, and so on. For this reason, there is NOT one set way of treating everyone under the same system, especially when possessing a different ROOT or SEED, without involving the Holy Trinity.

Plus, it is the Holy Spirit that reveals or pinpoints the inner SEEDS of negativity and weaknesses. For this reason, we must set aside our alone time with Him. While, at the same time, covering ourselves with the Blood of Jesus as our formal sacrifice for the Divine Information of Relativity.

What does Spiritual Relativity have to do with breaking yokes from the inside out? We need the Holy Spirit to unveil what relates to our psyche, period. If we do not go to the Source for help, our outsourcing method can become thwarted. According to scripture, it says, *"Likewise the Spirit also helps in our weaknesses. For we do not know what we should pray for as we ought, but the Spirit Himself makes intercession for us with groanings which cannot be uttered. Now He who searches the hearts knows what the mind of the Spirit is, because He makes intercession for the saints according to the Will of God."* Romans 8:26-27.

The truth of the matter is that if we do not follow Spiritual Protocol, *As It Pleases God*, with or without third-party intervention, we will develop some form of resistance. In most cases, this will prevent us from healing, according to our Divine Blueprint. Is the Holy Spirit considered a third party? It depends upon our perception of Him, but if we are ONE with the Holy Spirit, there is no need to consider Him as a go-between unless we choose to do so. To be clear, what I am speaking of here is a human form of third-party intervention without including the Holy Trinity in the equation.

Of course, we need people, and people need us. When dealing with *Courage: As It Pleases God*, they should not take the place of our Heavenly Relationship with the Holy Trinity. If we allow this to happen, we will run into secret or open resistance from the inside out. How do we know if we are dealing with some form of resistance? Listed below are a few examples, but not limited to such:

- ☐ We become resistant when we cannot control our tongue, saying anything without any form of reservation or restraint.

- ☐ We become resistant when consumed with the lusts of the flesh, the lust of the eyes, and the pride of life, while refusing to deal with the underlying reasons, conditioning, or traumas contributing to the lustful consummations.

- ☐ We become resistant when we want others to suffer. Or, we wish ill will upon another, especially when we cannot get what we want or when someone disagrees with us.

- ☐ We become resistant when we allow our inner chatter to run wild with negativity, jealousy, envy, and coveting, overruling our sense of good judgment.

- ☐ We become resistant when we find ourselves constantly playing mind games to manipulate, connive, bully, or prey on the weak, naive, and abandoned.

- ☐ We become resistant when we are dead-set on degrading others, dragging them through the mud, or kicking someone when they are down without encouraging, building, or lending a helping hand to pick them up.

- ☐ We become resistant when our ultimate goal is to use or rip people off to get what we want while always being on the TAKE. As a Word to the Wise, we must be on the GIVE to break any form of resistance.

- ☐ We become resistant when we are disrespectful, disobedient, and destructive, operating with tunnel vision without becoming a work-in-progress to create a win-win in all things.

- ☐ We become resistant when we are ungrateful, unforgiving, unrelenting, and hateful, complaining about everything or anyone without giving thanks for the simple things in life.

- ☐ We become resistant when we spit in the face of those who are genuinely helping us, when we bite the hand feeding us, or when we outright live in the past.

- ☐ We become resistant when we want help from others, yet we are unwilling to give help without any strings attached.

- ☐ We become resistant when we avoid adding the Holy Trinity into the equation of all things.

According to the Heavenly of Heavens, resistance in the Kingdom is a quick way to get barred or cut off. No one likes getting kicked to the curb, mainly when we rely on God to guide us in some way, shape, or form, be it known or unknown.

How can we avoid getting barred or cut off from Kingdom Access? We must surrender our will to the Will of God. What does this mean? When we give God what He wants, He will give us what we want or need, opening up the Kingdom of Heaven on our behalf. But, there is a catch! We must be willing and able to put our past behind us.

Holding on to the past creates unstable boulders, causing us to become unstable or unhinged, falling all over the place when shaken to the core. Or, we will find ourselves fighting tooth and nail to change the unchangeable, move the unmovable, and quench the unquenchable, declining Divine Intervention. Furthermore, if we do not pride ourselves on becoming rock-solid in our Kingdom Efforts, we will become tossed to and fro with the least amount of effort while having our Personal Power or *Courage* zapped.

Unbeknown to most, the secret or open loss of influence increases our resistance level as we become harder to deal with, talk to, or be around. Why? We may find ourselves doing a few things, but not limited to such:

☐ We will find ourselves complaining or criticizing with little or no understanding or compassion.

☐ We will find ourselves becoming judgmental control freaks or attempting to annihilate those we cannot control.

☐ We will find ourselves yelling, screaming, fussing, or fighting when frustrated, confused, fearful, helpless, or angry.

☐ We will find ourselves downplaying our flaws, habits, vices, or weaknesses to create a superficial image of superiority, or we may deflect our responsibility by playing the victim.

☐ We will find ourselves sabotaging all forms of relations by what we are saying, doing, or what we refuse to say or do out of selfishness, revenge, hatefulness, or unforgiveness.

As It Pleases God®: Book Series

☐ We will find ourselves looking for the negative instead of the win-win or positive.

☐ We will find ourselves talking to ourselves and others like a junkyard dog, distorting any image of goodness, faithfulness, or reliance.

☐ We will find ourselves underestimating ourselves and our Blessings while becoming dream killers or creativity distorters.

☐ We will find ourselves becoming consumed with jealousy, envy, pride, and greed, triggering the provokable weaknesses of others, digging ditches, playing tit-for-tat games, or engaging in some form of debauchery.

☐ We will find ourselves buying people, places, and things to fill a known or unknown void, circumventing some form of responsibility.

☐ We will find ourselves pilfering or bribing those who trust us, especially when our goal is to oppress without them realizing what is taking place until our yoking process is complete.

☐ We will find that we second-guess ourselves. Then again, we may make excuses to indulge in doing the wrong thing when we know the right thing to do, but choose temporary gratification instead.

Although we are all a work-in-progress, our soulish intent says all, regardless of how well we pretend or attempt to circumvent the truth. For this reason, there are certain things we should not play around with. What are they? Our character is one of them;

our fruits are the second, and our relationship with the Holy Trinity would be the third. The moment we can recognize our character and fruits, we are better able to take them to the Father, Son, and Holy Spirit for refining according to the Kingdom.

According to the Ancient of Days, if we ignore our character and fruits, wanting the Holy Trinity to do all the work, we are sadly mistaken. We must be willing to do our part in owning our truth and Spiritually Tilling our own ground, *As It Pleases God*.

So, my question is, 'How is it possible to repent regarding something we have yet taken the time to admit?' From a Kingdomly Perspective, it means repentance is not taking place as it should. Frankly, we can pray more, shake the roof off the house, read the Bible until we are blue in the face, go to Church every time the doors open, and have faith the size of a mountain. But if we do not REPENT, turning from our known or unknown wicked ways, it is like telling God we do not have any problems or issues within the human psyche.

When, in all actuality, an unrepentant heart leads us to *Playing Dirty* without us realizing it. Is this Biblical? Absolutely! *"And do you think this, O man, you who judge those practicing such things, and doing the same, that you will escape the judgment of God? Or do you despise the riches of His goodness, forbearance, and longsuffering, not knowing that the goodness of God leads you to repentance? But in accordance with your hardness and your impenitent heart you are treasuring up for yourself wrath in the day of wrath and revelation of the righteous judgment of God."* Romans 2:3-5.

Listen, if we fail to recognize the fruit or character traits we are dealing with from an earthly perspective, we allow denial and disobedience to set in. So, when it comes down to our Spiritual Fruits and Christlike Character, we become aloof, shifting the blame or responsibility to another. Or, there are times when we whitewash the truth to prevent some form of exposure from happening, especially when someone is holding our hidden secrets. For this reason, in the Kingdom, we require transparency.

To be clear, this does not mean we must expose our lives on Social Media or broadcast our skeletons publicly. It means that in the Kingdom, we must repentantly lay whatever it is on the Altar of God for Spiritual Regrafting or Renewal, *As It Pleases Him*.

The *Courage* of *Clean Playing* is about putting ourselves into Kingdom Perspective. What does this mean? We must view our lives according to Kingdom Standards, living as an example with the Fruits of the Spirit in hand, with Christlike Character at the forefront, while consistently owning our truth.

Plus, when we become a work-in-progress in this manner, if we make a mistake or fall short, we should be able to repentantly own up to it, doing a face-to-face with ourselves from the inside out. The moment we can honestly face ourselves on a moment-by-moment basis, our self-corrective efforts will assist us. How? Self-correcting, *As It Pleases God*, assists us in becoming better, stronger, wiser, consistent, and diligent without *Playing Dirty* to cover up what we need to come clean on.

Being an overcomer should cause us to want to assist others in doing likewise. If this innate ability does not kick in, we have work to do. Why? We are Blessed to be a Blessing, and if we are not able to see how we can become a Blessing to others without being a hindrance, we have work to do because something is clouding our sense of good judgment. What does this mean? Spiritual Blindness, Deafness, or Muteness is prevalent in our doings. Most often, it is due to some form of hidden jealousy, envy, pride, greed, coveting, or clout exposure.

What is clout exposure? When we pretend to be something we are not. Or, we fall under the Gifting, Calling, Talents, or Creativity of another without developing our own. Yet, we take it upon ourselves to hide the Spiritual Well, depriving others of having the same opportunity to glean where we are gleaning.

To be clear, we cannot hide our Spiritual Well for long; in due time, the Heavenly of Heavens must UNVEIL it to all in need of it, while depriving those who had the opportunity to share but selfishly did not do so. For example, with the Woman at the Well, if she had not shared what Jesus shared with her in John 4, due to the biases set forth by people, the internal Spiritual Well within her psyche would have run dry, causing her to continue to *Play Dirty*. Instead, she symbolically used her *Courage* from within to share a drink of water with Jesus. Then, she took the Spiritual Water or Living Water she received, sharing it with others, quenching their inner thirst as well.

What does *Playing Dirty* have to do with our Spiritual Well? When all is said and done, the Heavenly of Heavens wants us to know it has everything to do with sharing with others, regardless of whether we feel clean or dirty, good or bad, right or wrong, positive or negative, and righteous or unrighteous. Our *Hidden Gifts* from within, *As It Pleases God*, are often fused into the water we share to quench the natural thirst of another. As a part of our free will offering, regardless of what we serve another, we are accountable, period! Therefore, it behooves us to use the Fruits of the Spirit and Christlike Character to SERVE UP what is right and just in the Eye of God. If not, we become susceptible to our own devices.

www.DrYBur.com

Chapter Ten

HIDDEN GIFT

Self-Control has become an overlooked commodity designed to save our lives only if we just take the time to understand its invaluable lifesaving strategies. It is a GIFT from the Heavenly of Heavens, giving us the ability to save ourselves from self-destructing from the inside out. However, it is indeed one of the Fruits of the Spirit, requiring *Courage* to use *As It Pleases God*. Simply put, it takes Courage to say 'NO' and mean it. Yet, *Self-Control* holds all of the other Spiritual Fruits intact, especially if we learn how to use them correctly without becoming pompous.

We are often looking for the *Hidden Gift*s of God to be tangible; however, this one is so intangible, making the intangibilities of life tangible. More importantly, it is powerful enough to change our lives for the better, revamping the perception of those who yield to the *Wisdom of Self-Control*.

What is the purpose of *Self-Control* being a *Hidden Gift*? First and foremost, the same way Divine Wisdom is a Gift from the Heavenly of Heavens, unveiling the Secrets, Mysteries, and Principles of the Kingdom with the byproduct of Kingdom Favor. So is *Self-Control*, TAMING the secrets and mysteries of the human psyche. Secondly, it is also hidden because we must become AWARE and ADMIT what is going on within us to truly understand what is happening around us. Candidly, some cultures refuse to admit or talk about the traumatized psyche, continuing throughout life as if nothing happened. In turn, I refuse to become a victim of this sort of negligence, nor will I allow this to continue without doing my part, *As It Pleases God*, in helping another.

The worldly means of *Self-Control* work to a certain extent. On the other hand, by working it with *Courage: As It Pleases God* and using it as a Spiritual Fruit, we become a force to be reckoned with, especially if we are using all of the Fruits of the Spirit continuously and succinctly the way He intended. In this manner, not only does it become a Hidden Gift, but it also becomes our *Super Power* for our Heaven on Earth Experience!

Here is the deal: When omitting or denying *Self-Control*, we unknowingly pick up the character traits of a fool, a mocker, or the simple. Who am I to point the finger, right? To be clear, I am not pointing the finger; I am bringing forth a Spiritual Awareness that has the potential to take us to the next level in or out of the Kingdom. How is this possible? From a Spiritual Perspective, listed below are a few characteristics associated with the traits of a fool, a mocker, or the simple, but not limited to such:

- ☐ The *Fools* are considered unwise, reckless, abusive, disobedient, unteachable, habitual, negative, dull, stiff-necked, critical, unlistenable, boisterous about wrongdoings, excuse makers, justifiers, homewreckers, and so on. *"The fear of the LORD is the beginning of knowledge, but fools despise wisdom and instruction."* Proverbs 1:7.

- ☐ The *Mockers* are considered the bullies, control freaks, egotistical, brainwashers, ruthless, gossipers, negative contenders, competitors, braggers, and so on. *"But you, beloved, remember the words which were spoken before by the* apostles of our Lord Jesus Christ: how they told you that there would be mockers in the last time who would walk according to their own ungodly lusts. These are sensual persons, who cause divisions, not having the Spirit." Jude 1:17-19.

- [ ] The *Simple* is considered the naive, weak, easy prey, push-overs, influenceable, gullible, follower of acceptance, crowd-pleasers, constantly fearful, worryaholics, and so on. *"How long, you simple ones, will you love simplicity? For scorners delight in their scorning, and fools hate knowledge."* Proverbs 1:22.

Why do we need to know this information? Falling into these categories zaps our *Courage*, even if we pretend to be the best thing since sliced bread. Nonetheless, what happens behind closed doors determines the status of the psyche. How do I know? Here is what scripture has to say, *"Because they hated knowledge and did not choose the fear of the LORD, they would have none of my counsel and despised my every rebuke. Therefore, they shall eat the fruit of their own way, and be filled to the full with their own fancies. For the turning away of the simple will slay them, and the complacency of fools will destroy them; but whoever listens to me will dwell safely, and will be secure, without fear of evil."* Proverbs 1:29-33. *"The wise shall inherit glory, but shame shall be the legacy of fools."* Proverbs 3:35. For this reason, we do not want to waste our time bringing shame to our own names. So, let us go deeper.

The standalone word of 'Control' can mean a lot of things, but from a Spiritual Perspective, if we dissect it as such, it leads to us becoming a 'Con' or 'Troll' without us realizing it. The blaming game of deception, conning, and creating havoc in the lives of others has been around since the beginning of time, and nothing has changed. It has taken on a form of beguiled covering in a sophisticated form, causing us to miss our Spiritual Cues due to our lack of understanding.

As It Pleases God®: Book Series

The secret longing for Wisdom, *Courage*, and Control has not changed; yet, it is hidden within the human psyche, where it goes unnoticed but is prominently acted upon. According to Genesis 3:6-13, here is how it started, "*So when the woman saw that the tree was good for food, that it was pleasant to the eyes, and a tree desirable to make one wise, she took of its fruit and ate. She also gave to her husband with her, and he ate. Then the eyes of both of them were opened, and they knew that they were naked; and they sewed fig leaves together and made themselves coverings. And they heard the sound of the LORD God walking in the garden in the cool of the day, and Adam and his wife hid themselves from the presence of the LORD God among the trees of the garden. Then the LORD God called to Adam and said to him, 'Where are you?' So, he said, 'I heard Your voice in the garden, and I was afraid because I was naked; and I hid myself.' And He said, 'Who told you that you were naked? Have you eaten from the tree of which I commanded you that you should not eat?' Then the man said, 'The woman whom You gave to be with me, she gave me of the tree, and I ate.' And the LORD God said to the woman, 'What is this you have done?' The woman said, 'The serpent deceived me, and I ate.'*"

Unbeknown to most, once we omit interjecting SELF into the equation of CONTROL, we detach ourselves from conscious reasoning and Spiritual Absolutes. What does this mean? Amid the lack of internal control, we tend to find ourselves attempting to control the people, places, and things around us, most often without appreciating, understanding, or applying integral principles. Frankly, this is how we get the control freaks who will hurt, humiliate, abandon, or destroy those who do not fit into their circle of deception. Then again, they may use conning schemes for the sake of appearing *Courageous*.

According to the Heavenly of Heavens, this form of deception has plagued every family, and it is not going anywhere any time soon. In the meantime, we must understand and learn how to deal with it while casting down the vain imaginations associated with this underlying plague and interjecting *Self-Control*.

More importantly, we must be willing to discipline ourselves without fitting in with the crowd or going with the norm. Why?

As It Pleases God®: Book Series

Everyone has their own journey, be it Spiritual or not. So, whatever we must do to discipline our Earthen Vessels is for us to become better, stronger, and wiser, doing all things in the Spirit of Excellence with a work-in-progress demeanor. And then use it, them, or that to serve another by example. Here is a scripture to appreciate: *"Do you not know that those who run in a race all run, but one receives the prize? Run in such a way that you may obtain it. And everyone who competes for the prize is temperate in all things. Now they do it to obtain a perishable crown, but we for an imperishable crown. Therefore, I run thus: not with uncertainty. Thus, I fight: not as one who beats the air. But I discipline my body and bring it into subjection, lest, when I have preached to others, I myself should become disqualified."* Corinthians 9:24-27.

What is the purpose of developing *Self-Control*, especially when we have free will to do, say, and become whatever we like? We must incorporate the elements of righteousness; if not, we create a disservice to ourselves and our Bloodline. The undermining of our Spiritual Values has been compromised by worldliness.

How do we compromise ourselves? First, we are removing God from the equational efforts of our lives. Secondly, we are being fooled by those who are interjecting their own twang of deception, leading the innocent sheep to the slaughter or invoking rebellion within the human psyche. All of which causes us to fight against ourselves from within, spreading outwardly, while thinking we are at peace or that this is normal. What can we do to avoid compromising ourselves? Listed below are a few tips, but not limited to such:

- ☐ We cannot allow deception to shake us to the core, getting into our Mind, Body, Soul, and Spirit, causing us to become vulnerable, weak, a prime target, or crave attention of any kind.

    How do we protect ourselves, *As It Pleases God*? It is accomplished through safeguarding ourselves from the inside out by coming into Oneness with the Holy Trinity

(The Father, Son, and Holy Spirit) and knowing Who is in charge.

Spiritual Awareness of this magnitude is accomplished through the Word of God, prayer, repentance, forgiveness, fasting on occasion, meditating on the scriptures, or using positive affirmations, correcting the correctable with righteousness and positivity. *"Now, brethren, concerning the coming of our Lord Jesus Christ and our gathering together to Him, we ask you, not to be soon shaken in mind or troubled, either by spirit or by word or by letter, as if from us, as though the day of Christ had come."* 2 Thessalonians 2:1-2.

- ☐ We must pay attention to the fruits without attempting to judge, react, or justify. What does this mean? No one is perfect, but God gives us the ability to recognize a wolf in sheep's clothing by their fruits. Really? Yes, really!

  In the Garden of Eden, we were deceived by a fruit, and now the slivering effects of deception are known by its fruits as well, making us AWARE. Therefore, if we do not pay attention, we cannot lay the blame elsewhere, period! *"Let no one deceive you by any means; for that Day will not come unless the falling away comes first, and the man of sin is revealed, the son of perdition, who opposes and exalts himself above all that is called God or that is worshiped, so that he sits as God in the temple of God, showing himself that he is God."* 2 Thessalonians 2:3-4.

- ☐ We must pay attention to the signs of deception without reacting negatively or as if we do not have home training. If we exhibit the Fruits of the Spirit and Christlike Character, the deceptive measures will unveil themselves.

  On the other hand, if we stoop to their level, we thwart the revealing process. *"Do you not remember that when I was* still with you, I told you these things? And now you know what is restraining, that he may be revealed in his own time." 2 Thessalonians 2:5-6.

- ☐ We must pride ourselves on doing the right thing, putting the Holy Trinity at the forefront of our lives with every situation, circumstance, or event, while staying in the Light, shunning darkness. By far, this helps all things to work together for our good, regardless of how life may appear to the naked eye. *"For the mystery of lawlessness is already at work; only He who now restrains will do so until He is taken out of the way. And then the lawless one will be revealed, whom the Lord will consume with the breath of His mouth and destroy with the brightness of His coming."* 2 Thessalonians 2:7-8.

- ☐ We must stop lying to ourselves and others, priding ourselves on becoming and remaining transparently authentic, leaving little or no room for deception. Of course, no one is perfect; however, we must consciously and wholeheartedly try our best. *"The coming of the lawless one is according to the working of Satan, with all power, signs, and lying wonders, and with all unrighteous deception among those who perish, because they did not receive the love of the truth, that they might be saved."* 2 Thessalonians 2:9-10.

- ☐ We must work on ourselves daily, overcoming the lust of the eyes, the lust of the flesh, and the pride of life to develop *Self-Control*, ensuring we do not fall for pompous illusions. *"And for this reason, God will send them strong delusion, that they should believe the lie, that they all may be condemned who did not believe the truth but had pleasure in unrighteousness."* 2 Thessalonians 2:11-12.

- ☐ We must give *Thanks* in all things, regardless of our perception of them. If we allow God to receive the *'Glory'* out of all things, we are better able to discover the win-win that most people are oblivious to finding. *"But we are bound to give thanks to God always for you, brethren beloved by the Lord, because God from the beginning chose you for salvation through sanctification by the Spirit and belief in the truth, to which He called you by our gospel, for the obtaining of the glory of our Lord Jesus Christ."* 2 Thessalonians 2:13-14.

- ☐ We must not forget what the *Ancient of Ancients* left for us to glean to make us better, stronger, and wiser, *As It Pleases God* through Divine Wisdom. *"Therefore, brethren, stand fast and hold the traditions which you were taught, whether by word or our epistle."* 2 Thessalonians 2:15.

- ☐ We must not give up hope, working toward all things in the Spirit of Excellence. *"Now may our Lord Jesus Christ Himself, and our God and Father, who has loved us and given us everlasting consolation and good hope by grace, comfort your hearts and establish you in every good word and work."* 2 Thessalonians 2:16-17.

- ☐ We must be willing to pray amid all things, regardless of how they may appear to the naked eye or whether we use our inside or outside voice. If one needs help, ask. If one needs direction, ask. If one needs assistance, ask. *"Finally, brethren, pray for us, that the word of the Lord may run swiftly and be glorified, just as it is with you, and that we may be delivered from unreasonable and wicked men; for not all have faith."* 2 Thessalonians 3:1-2.

- ☐ We must believe God has our back without second-guessing Him or becoming anxious. *"But the Lord is faithful,* who will establish you and guard you from the evil one. And we have confidence in the Lord concerning you, both that you do and will do the things we command you. Now may the Lord direct your hearts into the love of God and into the patience of Christ. 2 Thessalonians 3:3-5.

☐ We must declutter the people, places, and things leading us away from the Kingdom. *"But we command you, brethren, in the name of our Lord Jesus Christ, that you withdraw from every brother who walks disorderly and not according to the tradition which he received from us. For you yourselves know how you ought to follow us, for we were not disorderly among you; nor did we eat anyone's bread free of charge, but worked with labor and toil night and day, that we might not be a burden to any of you, not because we do not have authority, but to make ourselves an example of how you should follow us."* 2 Thessalonians 3:6-9.

The *Hidden Gifts* of *Self-Control* are available to all, only maximized by a few Mentally, Physically, Emotionally, and Spiritually to invoke the Genius from within. When we indulge in righteousness WITHOUT *Self-Control*, our upright edifices are only an illusion.

Self-Control is a byproduct of righteousness, but it is not limited to righteousness. What does this mean? Anyone can use it for anything, with or without God. Blasphemy, right? Wrong. I have found more worldly people exhibiting more *Self-Control* in what they believe in, than Believers themselves. Therefore, we need to come off our high horses and squash this foolery!

My ear has been to the ground for a long time, and I am not here to sugarcoat anything or to appease anyone. Thus, the intended use of *Self-Control* has been manipulated to close our eyes to our reality. How? It is through justification and rationalization. Although *Self-Control* is a GIFT, it can also become a curse if we lack it, *As It Pleases God* to please ourselves.

Our unrighteousness reveals the uncontrollable elements of negativity of the inner man, regardless of the masks we assume. To be clear, this does not make someone a bad person; it means they may not have a complete understanding of the expectations of their Heaven on Earth Experience, or they may not have developed enough strength to say 'NO' to temptation.

Personally, back in the day, I was one of those people who did not have a clue about what God was expecting from me from the inside out. For this reason, I am not quick to judge another man's journey, knowing there is HOPE for all amid our Tests, Training, and Blessings, primarily if we apply ourselves according to Kingdom Principles and our Divine Blueprint. Instead, I lead by example, sharing the way to the Light or the equal opportunities of the Kingdom with much compassion and mercy.

More importantly, I help answer the Questionables of the Kingdom in a way that I wished someone had helped me back then. However, I do not discount my Spiritual Classroom; it has taught me about the Holy Trinity, the Kingdom, and our Heaven on Earth Experience that I would not have received any other way.

The *Spirit to Spirit* Relationship, along with Spiritual Principles, gives us the ability to self-correct amid whatever, whomever, and however, without self-destructing due to the lack of information, understanding, conditioning, or biases. In aligning this accordingly, *"And those who are Christ's have crucified the flesh with its passions and desires. If we live in the Spirit, let us also walk in the Spirit. Let us not become conceited, provoking one another, envying one another."* Galatians 5:24-26.

What if the Door of the Kingdom is not opening for us, especially when we are doing everything right? To be clear, this happens to everyone at some point to get our wheels turning in the correct direction or to steer us to the right path, according to our Predestined Blueprint. However, the Door of the Kingdom will remain closed for a few reasons, but not limited to such:

- ☐ We are not strong enough due to the lies we continue to tell ourselves, or we are in outright denial about something or someone.
- ☐ We are too gullible, weak, or lack understanding.
- ☐ We are indulging in the lust of the eyes, the lust of the flesh, or the pride of life, causing some form of Spiritual Blindness, Deafness, or Muteness.
- ☐ We are not exhibiting the Fruits of the Spirit and Christlike Character.
- ☐ We are not exhibiting humility, or our ego is getting the best of us.
- ☐ We are too angry, hateful, disrespectful, or rude.
- ☐ We are causing harm or trauma to the innocent, Mentally, Physically, Emotionally, or Spiritually.
- ☐ We are behaving selfishly, or our motives are wrong.
- ☐ We are unforgiving or revengeful.
- ☐ We are jealous, envious, greedy, or coveting.
- ☐ We are ungrateful, unrelenting, and conscienceless.
- ☐ We are asleep, Mentally, Physically, Emotionally, or Spiritually, not giving way to the Holy Trinity or the Kingdom of Heaven.

Why do we need to put in the effort? The Holy Spirit will not violate our free will; therefore, we must initiate Spiritual Relations. Why? Negative traits and behaviors are on the horizon without the Holy Spirit, even if we pretend to be Heaven-Sent. So, let us align this: *"But if you are led by the Spirit, you are not under the law. Now the works of the flesh are evident, which are: adultery, fornication, uncleanness, lewdness, idolatry, sorcery, hatred, contentions, jealousies, outbursts of wrath, selfish ambitions, dissensions, heresies, envy, murders, drunkenness, revelries, and the like; of which I tell you beforehand, just as I also told you in time past, that those who practice such things will not inherit the Kingdom of God."* Galatians 5:18-21.

If we have a desire to reverse the effects of negativity on any level, we must involve the Fruits of the Spirit and Christlike

Character. According to scripture, it says, "*But the Fruit of the Spirit is love, joy, peace, longsuffering (patience), kindness, goodness, faithfulness, gentleness, and self-control. Against such there is no law. And those who are Christ's have crucified the flesh with its passions and desires.*" Galatians 5:22-24. We can tiptoe around our Spiritual Fruits, but they do not lie; therefore, it is always best to work on them daily without denying or omitting the fallen or misdirected fruits.

The *Hidden Gifts* of *Self-Control* helps us to regraft the Root of our Spiritual Fruits. What if our Spiritual Fruits are perfect? All fruits, including the good, bad, and ugly, are subjected to Seedtime and Harvest. What does this mean? They need maintenance, time, harvesting, and pruning; therefore, we can never think we have arrived. If we do, we attract the TESTING of our fruits, or we will be thrown into a Spiritual Classroom called the Cycle of Life. So, if we are not suited up with the Whole Armor of God, we could be in for a rude awakening in more ways than one. For this reason, we need to work on ourselves, pray, and repent daily, ensuring the Holy of Holies are on our side, and we are not shaken to the core with the Vicissitudes of Life.

What is the big deal about *Self-Control*? It creates the DIVIDE. In so many words, it separates good and evil, right and wrong, just and unjust, light and darkness, positive and negative, and so on. The moment we cannot recognize the difference, we become Spiritually Blind, Deaf, or Mute to the point where everything begins to run together, creating some sort of blurred reaction, effect, or reality.

In addition, once consumed in such a manner, we will feel right in our own eyes as we give way to the lust of the eyes, the lust of the flesh, and the pride of life through some form of justification in the Name of God, and sometimes with '*The Devil Made Me Do It*' or '*God Told Me*' analogy. When, in all actuality, the voice we hear is our own inner chatter left ungoverned, uncorrected, and untamed, allowing the psyche to run wild, doing, saying, and instigating whatever and with whomever.

According to the Heavenly of Heavens, when we are on a path of destructive behavior, attitude, and character, leaving a trail of all types of victims, we symbolically dig a ditch for ourselves, regardless of how well we think we are on top of our game.

Spiritually, the moment innocent victims begin to cry out wholeheartedly, the Spirit of God must step in to see what is going on, assessing the damage or justification. In Biblical times, this is similar to what happened in Sodom and Gomorrah when the Angels came down to investigate the cries of the people. Here is the scripture, *"And the LORD said, 'Because the outcry against Sodom and Gomorrah is great, and because their sin is very grave, I will go down now and see whether they have done altogether according to the outcry against it that has come to Me; and if not, I will know.'"* Genesis 18:20-21.

In Genesis 19, in Sodom and Gomorrah, most would think this was just about sexual immorality when it was simply about *Self-Control* and the lack of love, respect for others, and the absence of people skills. What does this mean? They became 'Cons' or 'Trolls' with the lust of the eyes, the lust of the flesh, and the pride of life, allowing themselves to become consumed, Mentally, Physically, and Emotionally, without any form of repentance.

To add insult to injury, they were proud of their behavior, celebrating the victimization of another and drawing in the innocent or weak-minded into their lasciviousness, violating the free will of another. What is the big deal when having fun? To be clear, God loves us all, and there is nothing wrong with having fun. Plus, as consenting adults, we have free will to enjoy our lives how we desire, with whom we choose, and where. Still, we do not have the right to violate or assassinate the will of another, be it worldly or Spiritually!

So, *Self-Control* is very much needed in all areas of our lives to prevent God from putting a complete halt on us, wiping out our Bloodline, or turning us into a pillar of salt as He did with Lot's wife in Genesis 19:26. Why would this happen? Her heart was still in Sodom and Gomorrah, not focused on her family or the Will of God.

Listen to me, and listen well. Once God delivers us from something or someone or closes the Red Sea on our Egypt, we must exhibit *Courage* and *Self-Control* and not look back. Reminiscing about what He delivered us from or contemplating going back is an insult to God, making us appear ungrateful. As a result of wanting to go back to the Pit of lasciviousness, we will become cryptic or septic from the inside out. The bottom line is that regardless of how well we try to hide this condition from ourselves or others, we cannot hide it from God, the Holy Spirit, or the psyche. As a result, we become hardened or toxic while justifying our condition as a victim without realizing God gave us the victory.

Walking around with a hardened or toxic heart prevents us from living a fulfilled life, and it contaminates our Bloodline as well. How can we make this make sense with Lot's wife, especially after she turned into a pillar of salt? Due to her lack of *Self-Control*, her daughters became victims of this form of lack as well. How? They slept with their own father after getting him drunk to produce offspring. Here again, they violated his free will to get what they wanted. Really? Yes, really! Even animals instinctively know they cannot reproduce within their Bloodline—it creates a genetic taboo, causing known and unknown genetic defects.

Unfortunately, this generational curse loomed over Lot's family from the loss of the mother, spreading outwardly. Please allow me to Spiritually Align this story before going any further. *"Now the firstborn said to the younger, 'Our father is old, and there is no man on the earth to come in to us as is the custom of all the earth. Come, let us make our father drink wine, and we will lie with him, that we may preserve the lineage of our father.' So, they made their father drink wine that night. And the firstborn went in and lay with her father, and he did not know when she lay down or when she arose. It happened on the next day that the firstborn said to the younger, 'Indeed I lay with my father last night; let us make him drink wine tonight also, and you go in and lie with him, that we may preserve the lineage of our father.' Then they made their father drink wine that night* also. And the younger arose and lay with him, and he did not know when she lay down or when she arose. Thus, both the daughters of Lot were with child by their father. The firstborn bore a son and called his name Moab; he is the father of the Moabites to this day. And the younger, she also bore a son and called his name Ben-Ammi; he is the father of the people of Ammon to this day." Genesis 19:31-38.

In my opinion, not only did they lack *Self-Control*, but they lacked a conscience as well, creating strife and distortion within their Bloodline by default. How? This behavior did not happen by mistake; they were intentional, planning what they would do in advance without any form of shame attached. For me, it means they were accustomed to this behavior and did not see a problem with it, nor did their conscience convict them in any way.

If one has not noticed by now, these are the same people the Children of Israel were warring with. Yes, indeed, family strife at its best! They were cousins fighting against each other. How can we make this make sense? The Moabites and Ammonites were the descendants of Lot and his two daughters.

Moreover, we are not done yet! This saga takes us to the Wisest Man documented in the Bible, named King Solomon, the son of King David. What does this have to do with anything? Well, once again, it is family drama at its best. We are dealing with the lack of *Self-Control* that would turn a Wise Man into exhibiting traits of a fool, a mocker, or the simple. Blasphemy, right? Wrong! He inherited this lust from his father and mother, festering to another level when left untamed, unresolved, and ignored.

Here is the deal: In 1 Kings 11:1-2, it says, "*But King Solomon loved many foreign women, as well as the daughter of Pharaoh: women of the Moabites, Ammonites, Edomites, Sidonians, and Hittites—from the nations of whom the LORD had said to the children of Israel, 'You shall not intermarry with them, nor they with you. Surely they will turn away your hearts after their gods.' Solomon clung to these in love.*"

Sadly, King Solomon ignored the WISDOM of God and the teachings of his parents. How? He did not exhibit *Self-Control*, allowing the lust of the eye, the lust of the flesh, and the pride of life to consume his better judgment.

The longing of the human psyche is a force to be reckoned with, especially when power, money, sex, status, fame, and love are involved. Nevertheless, listed below are a few brewing GENERATIONAL CURSES and willful idolatry he allowed into his Bloodline, but not limited to such:

- ☐ He openly engaged in intermingling with his cousins, the Moabite and Ammonite women, the descendants of Lot, which continued the generational curses from Sodom and Gomorrah.

- ☐ He openly engaged in intermingling with his cousins, the Edomite women, the descendants of Esau, which continued the generational curse of disobedience.

- ☐ He openly engaged in intermingling with the Sidonian women, the descendants of Canaan, the grandson of Noah, linked to the generational curse of Canaan.

- ☐ He openly engaged in intermingling with the Hittite women, the descendants of Canaan, the son of Canaan, who is the grandson of Noah, linked once again to the generational curse of Canaan.

All in all, no one is immune to the negative impacts associated with the lack of *Self-Control* and generational curses. If we do not think generational curses are real, then think again! Now, to break any form of generational curse, we must control the flesh, and the bodily desires will go into dormancy.

Nevertheless, if we feed them, they will grow stronger with time, affecting our Bloodline with specific fruits or character flaws instead of Kingdom Benefits. More importantly, here is what yours truly, King Solomon, tells us in Proverbs 4:1-5: *"Hear, my children, the instruction of a father, and give attention to know understanding; for I give you good doctrine: do not forsake my law. When I was my father's son, tender and the only one in the sight of my mother, He also taught me, and said to me: Let your heart retain my words; keep my commands, and live. Get wisdom! Get understanding! Do not forget, nor turn away from the words of my mouth."*

We must cast down vain imaginations while teaching our family how to do likewise. If not, the penetration can become fierce, especially when we have to fight against our own for righteousness in the Eye of God. What does this mean? Our biggest enemy or most profound kryptonite is within us, our families, or those we know and have grown accustomed to being around. For example, when a child trusts and believes God for deliverance from a Bloodline Curse, and the parents continue to loom curses over the Divine Destiny of the child, it puts them into a Spiritual Gridlock instead of Spiritual Liberation.

What is a Spiritual Gridlock? Gridlock is when good parents are conditioned to parent their children how they were raised out of custom, not realizing they are under a generational curse. Due to the parents' negligence, the loomed curses are attempting to penetrate their offspring. As a result, they become Spiritually Weak, fighting against the secret or open curses of someone they love.

Everyone has their story, but with much respect to all, Spiritual Gridlock happens when the parents lack the understanding of 'What' they are doing or the damage it may cause to their offspring. Due to this oversight, a parent with good intentions never gets an understanding of '*Why*' they are cursing their own, '*How*' to become better, '*Where*' to go to receive help, and '*When*' to draw the line in the sand on their behaviors. As a result, the Bloodline Curse continues as a Spiritual Gridlock. Why? Their child became too traumatized to contend with the Stones of Wickedness, so they joined in to do likewise on their own, keeping the negative cycle going or becoming locked into the cycle.

From the Ancient of Ancients, if we do not unlock the negative debauched Grid, the lock will trap our Bloodline until someone steps up to the plate, saying 'NO MORE,' while regrafting their fruits from negative to positive, bad to good, unjust to just, wrong to right, cursed to blessed, and so on.

In the same way that a Negative Grid runs deep, a Spiritual Grid with the Fruits of the Spirit and Christlike Character runs deeper into the Well of Wisdom, Favoritism, Blessings, and Greatness. Really? Yes, really! Therefore, if we allow *Self-Control* to work on our behalf, there is no limit on what we can achieve, enabling our Bloodline to achieve even more.

Now, before ending this chapter, while writing it, I must admit there were all types of temptations pulling at me from everywhere, testing my level of *Self-Control* as well. Yet, I had to press through, enduring the vile attempts of the wolves in sheep's clothing without blowing my cover, ensuring this vital information gets to those in dire need of it.

But of course, I was not surprised; our fruits must be TESTED. It helps us avoid the problematic feelings of failure or having rotten fruits spoil the whole bunch of good fruits. How do we self-check our own fruits? We must involve the Holy Spirit in building ourselves from the inside out because He knows more about us than we do. Yet, here are the instructions from the Bible: *"But you, beloved, building yourselves up on your most holy faith, praying in the Holy Spirit, keep yourselves in the love of God, looking for the mercy of our Lord Jesus Christ unto eternal life."* Jude 1:20-21.

When using *Courage: As It Pleases God*, here is a Divine Word to keep close to the heart, especially when in a Spiritual Classroom or enduring the Vicissitudes of life, *"But He knows the way that I take; when He has tested me, I shall come forth as gold."* Job 23:10. By all means, repeat this scripture over and over. Even if layers of debris cover our gold, keep the faith, knowing: *"All things work together for good to those who love God, to those who are the called according to His purpose."* Romans 8:28.

Chapter Eleven

COURAGE

As a proclamation from the Heavenly of Heavens, every issue we have in life is based on selfishness, whether on our behalf or that of another. Although we are created in the Image of God, often enough, our charactorial fruits do not align with the intended purpose of the Kingdom. For this reason, we become caught up in areas where we should experience freedom. And then, we experience an illusion of freedom with people, places, and things that we should exercise extreme caution. So, this chapter aims to build *Courage: As It Pleases God*, illuminating our understanding of Spiritual Strength in ways superseding our worldly reasonings.

The bottom line is that we are in a worldly mix, being churned for defeat in areas we should RISE above in the Spirit of Greatness. However, while living life, we fail to know how to rise above our present situation or step outside of our comfort zone. Well, henceforth, according to the Ancient of Days, all is not lost. The long-awaited answers are woven within this chapter, transforming the *Least* to the *Greatest*. So, let us go deeper.

As It Pleases God®: Book Series

When going from the *Least* to the *Greatest*, the key to changing our lives, *As It Pleases God*, is within our reach. According to our Divine Blueprint, even if our lives do not appear as such right now, there is HOPE. Living an empty life is not something we would wish upon ourselves, yet it unknowingly happens too often. So, we must acclimate ourselves to revamp our thought process to accommodate the Will of God. If we take God out of the equation of our daily living, we will find ourselves doing, becoming, and saying things that contradict our Divine Blueprint without realizing it.

In stepping up to the plate with God in mind, we must get rid of a few things, but not limited to such:

- ☐ We must get rid of hatefulness, unforgiveness, and mercilessness.
- ☐ We must get rid of unhappiness, joylessness, or unappreciativeness.
- ☐ We must get rid of unrest, weariness, and worry.
- ☐ We must get rid of impatience or rushing all the time.
- ☐ We must get rid of unkindness, unforgiveness, or lack of compassion.
- ☐ We must get rid of evilness, cruelty, or any form of debauchery.
- ☐ We must get rid of unfaithfulness or doubtfulness.
- ☐ We must get rid of abrasiveness or rudeness.
- ☐ We must get rid of recklessness or disobedience.
- ☐ We must get rid of envy, jealousy, or covetousness.
- ☐ We must get rid of prideful arrogance.
- ☐ We must get rid of the lies, masks, and deception.

What is the purpose of getting rid of the above items? If we do not rid ourselves of specific negative characteristics, it will make us destitute and weak in the Realm of the Spirit. Even if we appear to have it all together, we subject ourselves to becoming a victim of worldliness if we willfully violate the human psyche.

Frankly, due to our lack of understanding in this area, we will find ourselves filling our inner voids with conditional items, superficial things catering to our senses, or pouncing on those appearing above or beneath us.

As the Heavenly of Heavens take note of our behaviors while assessing the core of man, we overlook many things, especially when we are getting what appears to be right in our own eyes but is deeply frowned upon in the Kingdom. When it is all said and done, we must consider the matters of the heart and our core values, regardless of our present state of being or how we feel about ourselves and others. To effectively regraft any form of negativity, we must pinpoint it first. What is the purpose of doing so? We cannot correct or regraft anything positively unless we know and understand 'What' it is first.

In the Kingdom, we cannot bypass the character-building steps for our Heaven on Earth developmental process. Nor can we neglect our people skills or the *Spirit to Spirit* Connection needed to tap into the Great Unknown. What is the purpose of doing so, especially when we are all grown up, and we are not children? Fortunately, we are all on a continuous learning curve, whether we admit it or not.

Plus, every charactorial trait we possess has a SEED, bearing much fruit, positively or negatively; therefore, we must deal with whatever or whomever according to the Standards of the Kingdom. If not, we can become swept away by our own devices or the tricks of the enemy. What does this mean for us, especially when we are giving or doing our best? We unawaringly set ourselves up for defeat due to our lack of understanding or our inability to deal with who we are from the inside out.

The human psyche is a force to be reckoned with in or out of the Realm of the Spirit. Why? First and foremost, we are Spiritual Beings subjected to human trauma, conditioning, adaptation, or regrafting. Secondly, the human psyche seeks to control our Mind, Body, and Spirit, affecting our external manifestations through our senses, feelings, and lusts. And thirdly, it has the desire to rewrite our Divine Blueprint, causing us to symbolically jump the track in our thoughts, emotions, and character, creating rotten fruits and reproducing after its own kind.

We can pretend not to be affected by the psyche. But the truth is, we are all affected in some way. Thus, we must understand that we are all a work-in-progress with weaknesses in need of regrafting. Most often, our Blessings are wrapped in our weaknesses. If we do not unwrap the negative seeds feeding it, we will miss the mark, giving our psyche the power to run the show. Once this happens, it will cause us to play pretend or assume all types of superficial masks to appear Godly or Heaven Sent, especially when we are doing the do or playing dirty. Meanwhile, in the Eye of God, we are one step away from exploding outwardly or imploding inwardly.

In all-knowing from the Heavenly of Heavens, the first step to assuming our rightful place in the Kingdom is to develop DISCIPLINE. If we are developing a deaf ear to the Will or Ways of God, swinging it high and low, we are definitely out of order. Who am I to judge, right? I am the mere Messenger from the Heavenly of Heavens, bringing forth the instructions needed for such a time as this.

Yet, before we move on, let us align this accordingly. We first hear about this in Genesis 32, during the molded calf incident with the Children of Israel. However, this is the scripture we must take note of: "*And the LORD said to Moses, 'Go, get down!' For your people whom you brought out of the land of Egypt have corrupted themselves. They have turned aside quickly out of the way which I commanded them. They have made themselves a molded calf, and worshiped it and sacrificed to it, and said, 'This is your god, O Israel, that brought you out of the land of Egypt!' And the LORD said to Moses, 'I have seen this people, and indeed it is a stiff-necked people!'* " Genesis 32:7-9.

In all actuality, in today's day and age, it is rude to call someone stiff-necked, dull, or wayward, especially an elder, because we all possess these character traits. However, when dealing with *Courage: As It Pleases God*, it is NOT rude to self-correct this negative characteristic from the *Least* to the *Greatest* or from the *Youngest to the Eldest.*

In the same way that Moses pleaded with God on behalf of the Children of Israel, we can do likewise with ourselves first and then with others. But, if we do it with the Holy Spirit and the Blood of Jesus, it creates a Spiritual Seal, helping us to help ourselves and our Bloodline. What do our Bloodlines have to do with anything? We do not want this characteristic to transfer without the correct KNOW-HOW in dealing with it on a moment-by-moment basis and on any Spiritual Level.

What do levels have to do with anything? In the Kingdom, it has everything to do with it. From a Spiritual Perspective, if we know nothing about God, the penalty is not as harsh as those who are Spiritually Seasoned or Marked, knowing better and willfully choosing not to do better. What is the big deal, and are we not all equal? Disobedience in the Eye of God is not something we want to play around with or proclaim equal rights, especially when this is a SORE SPOT for Him from the Garden of Eden Experience.

Nevertheless, if we want to throw around equal rights in the Kingdom, then let us royally break this down. Disobedience is disobedience, right? Of course, it is! But if we have seen or experienced the Divine Miracles of God, time after time, and still choose to spit in His face, do we think this is equal? Do we? Can we make this make sense to ourselves? Do we think God is a joke?

When playing with God like this without repentance, we will see His Divine Wrath so fast it will make our heads spin. Why? First, we belong to Him, and He is a Jealous God. More importantly, we can read all about '*Why*' He is jealous in Genesis 34. Secondly, when we take from a Spiritual Well with deceitfulness to unjustifiably manipulate, hurt, abuse, or cast down another without correcting the divisive attempts or repentance, we become the enemy of God. What are the attempts? To replace God Almighty with worldliness or vain imaginations for our selfish pleasures or gain.

When we properly equip ourselves to deal with disobedience, we are less likely to create golden calves to replace our invisible God of the Heavenly of Heavens. Yet, if we do, in due time, He will strip us, Mentally, Physically, Emotionally, or Spiritually. Really? Yes, really. Then, we will find ourselves covering our nakedness with tangible stuff without using the intangible Blood of Jesus as a Spiritual Covering.

Suppose we do not want our nakedness exposed. In this case, we must willfully and humbly repent, turning from all forms of debauchery and developing a *Spirit to Spirit* Relationship, using the Fruits of the Spirit and behaving Christlike. Why? God does not like people, places, and things taking His place, especially when He is the Creator of it all and Who is within us all. Let us interject scripture before moving on. "*Go up to a land flowing with milk and honey; for I will not go up in your midst, lest I consume you on the way, for you are a stiff-necked people. And when the people heard this bad news, they mourned, and no one put on his ornaments. For the LORD had said to Moses, 'Say to the children of Israel, you are a stiff-necked people. I could come up into your midst in one moment and consume you. Now therefore, take off your ornaments, that I may know what to do to you.' So, the children of Israel stripped themselves of their ornaments by Mount Horeb.*" Genesis 33:3-6.

Amid all, we must do our due diligence in all things Spiritual. What does this mean? We must pride ourselves in using the Fruits of the Spirit, exhibiting Christlike Character, and involving the Holy Trinity in the equation. By far, this does help us to self-correct instead of self-destructing. Here is what we need to know: "*So Moses made haste and bowed his head toward the earth, and worshiped. Then he said, 'If now I have found grace in Your sight, O Lord, let my Lord, I pray, go among us, even though we are a stiff-necked people; and pardon our iniquity and our sin, and take us as Your inheritance.' And He said: Behold, I make a covenant. Before all your people I will do marvels such as have not been done in all the earth, nor in any nation; and all the people among whom you are shall see the work of the LORD. For it is an awesome thing that I will do with you. Observe what I command you this day.*"

As It Pleases God®: Book Series

Behold, I am driving out from before you the Amorite and the Canaanite and the Hittite and the Perizzite and the Hivite and the Jebusite. Take heed to yourself, lest you make a covenant with the inhabitants of the land where you are going, lest it be a snare in your midst." Genesis 34:8-12.

According to the Heavenly of Heavens, we block our own Blessings by doing our own thing, becoming ungrateful, selfish, arrogant, and disobedient as if we are the Supreme Being, ruling over all things.

How do we know if we are blocked? If we do not possess that which money cannot buy, then we must do a check-up from the neck up. What can money not buy? It cannot buy God, the Holy Spirit, the Blood of Jesus, the Fruits of the Spirit, and Christlike Character. In addition, listed below are a few other items, but not limited to such:

- ☐ Our money cannot buy inner serenity of peace, comfort with God, ourselves, and others for edification, *Self-Control*, and a direct connection to the Realm of the Spirit. Nor can it help us invoke supernatural faith, uncommon favor, or the unique, fashionable style of our Divine Blueprint.

- ☐ Our money cannot buy inner charactorial conviction or correction with justifiable truths hidden in the power of *Repenting, Forgiving, Fasting, and Praying.*

- ☐ Our money cannot buy inner guidance with a grid-worthy distinction, making the Word of God applicable to our daily living in or out of our *Divine Anointing.*

- ☐ Our money cannot buy the empowerment of our Inner Genius, overriding or nullifying our *Toxic Influences.*

- ☐ Our money cannot buy the ANOINTING of our Gifts, Talents, Calling, Creativity, or Fruits. Nor can it

UNVEIL our Spiritual Eyes, Ears, and Mouth to obtain our Kingdom Credentials.

- ☐ Our money cannot buy the guidance of the Ready Writer from within. Nor can it buy or *Strategize* our Plan of Action or our next move relating to the FULL PORTION of our Divine Blueprint without Spiritual Guidance.

- ☐ Our money cannot buy the Inner Revelation of the Great Unknown, unveiling our *Spiritual Folds*.

- ☐ Our money cannot buy the unspeakable inner joy, quenching thirsts, or pangs of hunger within the human psyche.

- ☐ Our money cannot buy the Infallible Teacher in or out of our *Q and A Sessions* or Spiritual Classroom.

- ☐ Our money cannot buy the inner or outer voice of Divine Utterance, Reasoning, Prophecy, or Intercession.

- ☐ Our money cannot buy the gifted spark of genuine creativity, wisdom, and knowledge from God's Perspective.

- ☐ Our money cannot buy Spiritual Illumination, unveiling the elements of our *Eternal Life* now.

Clearly, money can provide a comfortable lifestyle with tangible stuff; however, if we do not master the intangibles, *As It Pleases God*, the tangibles will not matter after we adapt to them or endure the traumas associated. Here is what we must know when building *Courage: As It Pleases God*, and why we need to obtain what money cannot buy.

- "*Hell and Destruction are never full; So the eyes of man are never satisfied.*" Proverbs 27:20.

- "*The righteous eats to the satisfying of his soul, But the stomach of the wicked shall be in want.*" Proverbs 13:25.

- "*For the eyes of the greedy man are never satisfied; He heaps up wealth for himself, But does not know who will gather it.*" Ecclesiastes 4:8.

- "*But those who desire to be rich fall into temptation and a snare, and into many foolish and harmful lusts which drown men in destruction and perdition.*" 1 Timothy 6:9.

- "*The leech has two daughters—Give and Give! There are three things that are never satisfied, Four never say, 'Enough!': The grave, The barren womb, The earth that is not satisfied with water—And the fire never says, 'Enough!'*" Proverbs 30:15-16.

If we downplay or omit the Holy Trinity in our daily living, it may cause us to doubt ourselves, creating a vicious cycle of déjà vu, self-sabotage, or self-righteousness. Why? We are created to learn from anything and everyone, deciphering through the information, choosing the positive, and discarding the negative to create a win-win. And if we are Spiritually Blind, Deaf, or Mute, we will begin to miss out on the simple things in life. In addition, doubt will unawaringly become our motivating factor, creating all types of known and unknown Spiritual disasters. Then again, they may cause us to become accident-prone.

As It Pleases God, the inner workings of the Spirit are not for sale, not now and not ever! It is through GRACE and MERCY that God withholds His wrath. But let us align this: "*Therefore, understand that the LORD your God is not giving you this good land to possess because of your righteousness, for you are a stiff-necked people.*

'Remember!' Do not forget how you provoked the LORD your God to wrath in the wilderness. From the day that you departed from the land of Egypt until you came to this place, you have been rebellious against the LORD." Deuteronomy 9:6-7.

Listen, if we dare to align our lives with the Word of God, we will find our lives becoming better and strategically aligned with our Divine Blueprint. With all due respect, we often find ourselves not understanding the Bible to the fullest because we are Spiritually Asleep. Therefore, we must AWAKEN our Spirit to become One with the Holy Spirit, covering ourselves with the Blood of Jesus, and repenting consistently. How is this possible? It helps us to MIRROR our lives, giving us a reflection through the Eye of God, as well as the eyes of man. Plus, it helps to tame the human psyche, ensuring it stays respectful and in its rightful place.

How can a Biblical Mirror help us? If we take the Bible, asking the right fact-finding questions related to us personally, we can better understand how it provides the Spiritual Therapy that money cannot buy. Blasphemy, right? Wrong! When dealing with the human psyche, we must know the Spiritual Principles of God to avoid creating Spiritual Taboos in our Bloodline, playing ourselves short, or playing mind games, causing us to become played in the end. How does this work? Although we are all different, listed below are a few pointers helping us to get started, but not limited to such:

- ☐ We must be willing to step into the Spiritual Classroom with the Holy Trinity (The Father, Son, and Holy Spirit) in charge.

- ☐ We must be willing to pray, repent, fast, and meditate on the Word of God, while using positive affirmations as well.

- ☐ We must engage in a *Spirit to Spirit* Connection in our alone time, perfecting our Spiritual Vision, Hearing, and Language.

- ☐ We must document what we are Spiritually Seeing, Hearing, and Speaking with our inside voice.

- ☐ We must ask fact-finding questions when reading the Bible, extracting 'What' happened, 'Why' it happened, 'Where' it happened, 'When' it could happen to us, 'How' to deal with it or overcome, and with 'Whom' to attract, avoid, share, build up, or cast down.

- ☐ We must replace negativity with positive affirmations or scriptures, counteracting any form of evil or waywardness.

- ☐ We must get rid of any form of disobedience or rebellion that takes us out of the Will of God.

- ☐ We must question our behavior by aligning it with the Fruits of the Spirit consistently.

- ☐ We must pride ourselves on exhibiting Christlike Character, even when things are not going our way or people are treating us like junkyard dogs.

- ☐ We must be willing to stick to the Promises of God, even when we cannot see our way through.

- ☐ We must listen, learn, grow, and sow back into the Kingdom of God when called upon.

- ☐ We must be willing to pursue righteousness, even if worldliness becomes very tempting to our senses, habits, and lusts.

Now, before we go any further, let us align: "*Take this Book of the Law, and put it beside the ark of the covenant of the LORD your God, that it may be there as a witness against you; for I know your rebellion and your stiff neck. If today, while I am yet alive with you, you have been rebellious against the LORD, then how much more after my death? Gather to me all the elders of your tribes, and your officers, that I may speak these words in their hearing and call heaven and earth to witness against them.*" Deuteronomy 31:26-28.

What is the big deal about stiff necks? Disobedience leads to some form of idolatry, regardless of whether we admit it or not. For this reason, we do not want this to pass on to our children or children's children. However, if this charactorial SEED has been passed to us, it is our responsibility to regraft it positively. Here is what the Bible has to say: "*Yet the LORD testified against Israel and against Judah, by all of His prophets, every seer, saying, 'Turn from your evil ways, and keep My commandments and My statutes, according to all the law which I commanded your fathers, and which I sent to you by My servants the prophets.' Nevertheless, they would not hear, but stiffened their necks, like the necks of their fathers, who did not believe in the LORD their God.*" 2 Kings 17:13-14.

How will obedience benefit us? It helps us to break known or unknown yokes, bondages, and generational curses, preventing us from becoming captives of ourselves or of another. What does this mean? We are often our biggest enemy from the inside out based on our thoughts, actions, beliefs, reactions, behaviors, words, lack of conscience, fruits, and character traits. The enemy from within subjects us to becoming the enemy of another, keeping the cycle of deception or lies going. Although no one is perfect, we must become accountable for what is happening inside us, spreading outwardly, affecting, infecting, or traumatizing others, especially the innocent.

In our Union of Oneness, it behooves us to engage in private sessions with God, developing our *Spirit to Spirit* Connection as a form of exercise for the conscience. What can this do for us? It will help develop our Spiritual Senses, Fruits, and Character.

Plus, it assists in revamping our psyche to become merciful, forgiving, gracious, unselfish, and compassionate when others are judging and condemning or being greedy, selfish, prideful, competitive, and covetous.

Here is what we need to glean, As It Pleases God: "*Now do not be stiff-necked, as your fathers were, but yield yourselves to the LORD; and enter His sanctuary, which He has sanctified forever, and serve the LORD your God, that the fierceness of His wrath may turn away from you. For if you return to the LORD, your brethren and your children will be treated with compassion by those who lead them captive, so that they may come back to this land; for the LORD your God is gracious and merciful, and will not turn His face from you if you return to Him.*" 2 Chronicles 30:8-9.

Unbeknown to most, disobedience creates Spiritual Delays in our developmental process. From my perspective, this is similar to being held back a grade in school, but in the Spiritual Classroom with a cycle of déjà vu. When a situation, circumstance, or event keeps repeating itself, it is imperative to look at the root cause of the matter. Why? There is a SEED, and if we overlook it, it will continue to reproduce after its own kind. What does this mean? We cannot expect a different type of fruit with the same Seed.

According to the Spiritual Law of Seedtime and Harvest, Seeds will produce the fruits of likeness in different situations until we learn the lesson, regraft the root, or prune whatever or whomever. At the same time, the Root of Disobedience is NOT a fruit that we want to feed continuously. Why? The Spiritual Taboos associated have the potential to run deep into our lineage, annihilating our Bloodline or invoking a generational curse, especially if we give in to haughtiness.

What does haughtiness have to do with our Bloodline? Unbeknown to most, this sort of bull's eye is placed upon two types of people, primarily if they are not extremely careful:

- ☐ The Boastful.
- ☐ The Wicked.

For this one, I do not wish upon my worst enemy; therefore, allow me to take it to scripture. *"I said to the boastful, 'Do not deal boastfully,' and to the wicked, 'Do not lift up the horn. Do not lift up your horn on high; Do not speak with a stiff neck.' For exaltation comes neither from the east nor from the west nor from the south. But God is the Judge: He puts down one, and exalts another."* Psalm 75:4-7. Who is protected from this bull's eye? The opposite category can justifiably invoke protection over their Bloodline without praying amiss, which are:

- ☐ The Humble.
- ☐ The Righteous.

To be clear, this does not mean perfection; it is willful and workable humility and fully repenting or authentic righteousness. More importantly, here is what we need to know: *"All the horns of the wicked I will also cut off, but the horns of the righteous shall be exalted."* Psalm 75:10. For this reason, before we toot our horns on any level, it is imperative to know and understand our antonyms.

Why do we need to know antonyms when dealing with Spirituality? When approaching *Courage: As It Pleases God*, knowing our opposites helps us counteract negatives with positives, evil with good, unjust with just, wrong with right, and so on. When we fail to understand the differences, we can become easily deceived, confused, misunderstood, and frustrated in our communicative efforts.

The minute we are unable to counteract positively, we become susceptible to the wiles of the enemy because *"Those who live according to the flesh set their minds on the things of the flesh, but those who live according to the Spirit, the things of the Spirit."* Romans 8:5. Listed below are a few susceptibilities when the Holy Spirit is NOT present, but not limited to such:

- [ ] We will revert to the path of least resistance or become increasingly lazy. *"The lazy man buries his hand in the bowl; it wearies him to bring it back to his mouth. The lazy man is wiser in his own eyes than seven men who can answer sensibly."* Proverbs 26:15-16.

- [ ] We will let our guards down, downplaying our instinctual nature while becoming hateful from the inside out. *"He who hates, disguises it with his lips, and lays up deceit within himself."* Proverbs 26:24.

- [ ] We become less likely to convert or look for a win-win due to our hidden inner defeats. *"Whoever has no rule over his own spirit is like a city broken down, without walls."* Proverbs 25:28.

- [ ] We will show our true selves with zero accountability while playing the blaming game, digging deep ditches, or setting traps out of spite. *"Whoever digs a pit will fall into it, and he who rolls a stone will have it roll back on him."* Proverbs 26:27.

- [ ] We become prone to jealousy, envy, and coveting, contributing to our own slumber. *"Do not be envious of evil men, nor desire to be with them; for their heart devises violence, and their lips talk of troublemaking."* Proverbs 24:1-2.

- [ ] We will constantly have a bout with ungratefulness, contention, and greediness. *"It is better to dwell in a corner of a housetop, than in a house shared with a contentious person."* Proverbs 25:24.

- [ ] We are less likely to forgive, having mercy upon another without instigating some form of ruckus. *"He who sends a message by the hand of a fool cuts off his own feet and drinks* violence. Like the legs of the lame that hang limp is a proverb in the mouth of fools. Like one who binds a stone in a sling is he who gives honor to a fool." Proverbs 26:6-8.

- [ ] We are prone to wallowing as a victim or becoming a talebearer. "The words of a talebearer are like tasty trifles, and they go down into the inmost body." Proverbs 26:22.

- [ ] We become a magnet for confusion, chaos, and debauchery. "The great God who formed everything gives the fool his hire and the transgressor his wages. As a dog returns to his own vomit, so a fool repeats his folly." Proverbs 26:10-11.

- [ ] It becomes challenging to develop or maintain a Positive Mental Mindset as we become bombarded by the Vicissitudes of Life, feeling right in our own eyes. "Do you see a man wise in his own eyes? There is more hope for a fool than for him." Proverbs 26:12.

- [ ] It becomes easier to player-hate or meddle while developing loose lips, saying and doing anything, or operating without a conscience. "He who passes by and meddles in a quarrel not his own is like one who takes a dog by the ears. Like a madman who throws firebrands, arrows, and death, is the man who deceives his neighbor, and says, 'I was only joking!'" Proverbs 26:17-19.

- [ ] It becomes easier to compete in or out of our field of expertise while finding fault in others or negatively outing them for developing their Gifts, Calling, Talents, Creativity, or being in Purpose on purpose. "Debate your case with your neighbor, and do not disclose the secret to another; lest he who hears it expose your shame, and your reputation be ruined." Proverbs 25:9-10.

If we wet our whistles with the Word of God instead of tooting our own horns, we are better able to contend on a level most cannot. What is the big deal about tooting our own horns? Although we use positive affirmations to build ourselves up in Earthen Vessel, pompousness will not get it, especially when the enemy is ready to make an example out of us. However, here is what the scripture has to say to us, *"Do not boast about tomorrow, for you do not know what a day may bring forth. Let another man praise you, and not your own mouth; a stranger, and not your own lips."* Proverbs 27:1-2.

Even if we cannot quickly rebound, we have the Word of God as our point of refuge until we develop and strengthen our Spiritual Muscles or Wings of Righteousness. Is this Biblical? Of course, it says, *"For to be carnally minded is death, but to be spiritually minded is life and peace. Because the carnal mind is enmity against God; for it is not subject to the law of God, nor indeed can be. So then, those who are in the flesh cannot please God. But you are not in the flesh but in the Spirit, if indeed the Spirit of God dwells in you. Now if anyone does not have the Spirit of Christ, he is not His. And if Christ is in you, the body is dead because of sin, but the Spirit is life because of righteousness."* Romans 8:6-10.

What is the purpose of building ourselves from the inside out? We must build ourselves Mentally, Physically, Emotionally, and Spiritually. The Bible tells us to *"Prepare your outside work, make it fit for yourself in the field; and afterward build your house."* Proverbs 24:27. When omitting the building process from the inside out, we will break easily amid the Vicissitudes of Life or when placed under pressure, forcing us to get out of character instead of putting on the Whole Armor of God.

Operating with *Courage: As It Pleases God*, we must deal with the human psyche through Spiritual Means to apply Divine Wisdom. Using this Spiritual Approach, *As It Pleases Him*, assists in dealing with worldliness without running for cover with our tail in between our legs as if He is not on the Throne.

As It Pleases God®: Book Series

Why would we run as if God is not God? Most often, it is out of fear, doubt, lack of understanding, or immaturity. However, it is *"Through wisdom a house is built, and by understanding it is established; by knowledge the rooms are filled with all precious and pleasant riches. A wise man is strong, Yes, a man of knowledge increases strength; for by wise counsel you will wage your own war, and in a multitude of counselors there is safety."* Proverbs 24:3-6.

We are designed to make a difference for ourselves and those who are following suit. For this reason, we must take our lives seriously, making the most out of everything and with everyone, as we become a Fountain of Wisdom, as our Spiritual Portions run over. When overflowing with *Courage* in such a manner, Blessings will follow us everywhere we go.

For example, a person possessing the Spirit of Overflow can walk into a business where it is so slow with little or no customers. Then, all of a sudden, there is an influx of customers coming in to patronize this business. To be clear, this is not a one-time overflow; it is a constant overflow of Blessings following this individual, spilling over onto anyone around them as well.

Now, on the other side of the coin, we must also exercise caution around those who are a magnet to curses, evil, scattering, negativity, chaos, and so on. Listen, the gravitational pull does not lie; therefore, we must exercise extreme caution or quickly get to the root of the matter. Why? Energy is transferable, especially if we are weak, sick, traumatized, or inexperienced. For this reason, our Spiritual Instinct must be up to par, knowing when to hold, fold, or walk away; if not, in the next chapter, the *Unveiled Queries* will help us in this process.

Before ending this chapter on *Courage: As It Pleases God*, here is the Spiritual Decree and Seal: *"I announce to you today that you shall surely perish; you shall not prolong your days in the land which you cross over the Jordan to go in and possess. I call heaven and earth as witnesses today against you, that I have set before you life and death, blessing and cursing; therefore choose life, that both you and your descendants may live;*

that you may love the LORD your God, that you may obey His voice, and that you may cling to Him, for He is your life and the length of your days; and that you may dwell in the land which the LORD swore to your fathers, to Abraham, Isaac, and Jacob, to give them." Deuteronomy 30:18-20.

Chapter Twelve

UNVEILED QUERIES

Our *Unveiled Queries* give us the *Courage* to dig a little deeper without having to whitewash or compete with the people, places, and things needed to help us get to the next level. What is more, it helps keep the mind from wandering off into places it should not entertain. Unbeknown to most, without *Courage*, discontentment, insecurity, and hidden thirsts, keeps the mind in the *'What If,'* *'When I become,'* or *'Only If'* status.

We can tiptoe around whether or not we are *Courageous*, but it is revealed in our fruits and character traits. The moment we speak, we become a tell-all book, especially among those who have done their homework in the Realm of the Spirit; therefore, we must take responsibility, period!

The lack of accountability is one of the most significant issues we face today. Still, the unfortunate thing about it is that most often, we are unaware of it, especially if we do not ask ourselves the right fact-finding questions, *As It Pleases God*. Yet, we are quick to question others without taking the time to *Query* the human psyche or what lies within.

Unbeknown to most, our psyche will protect itself, doing whatever it likes until it is put on blast, in the same way that we are prone to put others on blast when they get our time wrong. So, in this chapter, we will *Unveil* the *Veiled* to ensure we understand the Spiritual Protocols needed to take our mindset from negative to Kingdom. At the same time, we put a damper on what we do not understand while bringing forth our Highest and Best Self.

The *Unveiled Queries* that we do not have with ourselves usually keep us held up or held back from the inside out. Even though we may appear or feel as if we have it all together, the truth is that we are all a work-in-progress. We are all in need of Spiritual Restoration with our Fruits of the Spirit and our Christlike Character. What does this mean? Most often, we proclaim to be a Child of the Most High God. Still, our behaviors, thoughts, emotions, attitudes, or charactorial traits do not align with what God has in mind, especially when it comes down to Kingdom Principles.

Better yet, we even have those proclaiming to be Believers hurling curses over the innocent without realizing the implications of what they are doing. Due to this form of Spiritual Negligence, when we have unreconcilable differences and insecurities hidden within the human psyche, or when we feel offended in some way based upon untruths or self-induced truths, we attempt to assassinate others Spiritually.

How is this possible as Believers? We have often become unantiquated in our approach to Spirituality, or we do not understand the Spiritual Laws and Protocols set in motion to protect all things Spiritual. As a result, we get caught up in our self-induced web of deception. And then, we cannot understand how life is serving us a bad hand, primarily when the *Gravitational Pull* of Life will not lie.

Unbeknown to most, life is designed to make our lives easier when we use the Spiritual Principles associated with the Divine Blueprint already set in place. Once we go against them, doing our own or the wrong things, we will find our lives becoming rugged and resistant. It is like a rubber band, attempting to pull us back into our natural alignment. If we continue to resist, the band will break, leaving us to our own devices as we become out of control, reckless, ungrateful, and defiant. Then, as a slap in the face, we sometimes use Spirituality as a form of guise to cover up our unrighteousness instead of dealing with it.

The time has come for us to stop lying to ourselves about our attitude, behaviors, demeanor, pullback, or how we deal with each other. What is the big deal? The big deal resides in the lies permeating the Culture of the Kingdom, especially when everyone wants to be so Spiritual or Godly without proper representation. What does this mean? Unfortunately, this is when we proclaim to be in the Kingdom; yet, we do not take the time to seriously work on our fruits, character, attitude, behavior, etiquette, or countenance. While, at the same time, thinking this is okay in the Eye of God or laying the blame elsewhere.

For the record, contrary to what we are being taught, misbehaving is highly frowned upon in the Kingdom. Listed below are a few examples, helping us to pinpoint the erring process, but not limited to such:

- ☐ A nasty, hateful, or rude person usually does not realize they are rude, abrasive, or disrespectful, nor do they admit to behaving in such a manner.

- ☐ An abusive or traumatizing individual does not own up to their behavior, so they feel there is no need to change because they somehow feel justified.

- ☐ An evil person feels right in their own eyes, thinking everyone has a problem without admitting their contribution to such debauchery.

- ☐ A backstabber or competitor does not realize they are bound by the hidden elements of jealousy, envy, pride, and coveting.

- ☐ A chaotic individual thinks their form of communication works for everyone without realizing or recognizing the traumatized victims they are leaving behind.

- ☐ A controlling manipulator does not realize or acknowledge that everyone is entitled to their own opinion and free will.

- ☐ A firestarter or talebearer does not acknowledge the trail of innocent victims they have burned, Mentally, Physically, Emotionally, and Spiritually, or who they have outright destroyed for fun. This is also applicable to playing one person against another, similar to playing one parent against another, one child against the next, one friend against the other, and so on, to get what we want.

  As a forewarning from the Heavenly of Heavens, it is an atrocity to have a parent or child torn from the inside out for putting one over another. This harmful tactic is written all over the Bible, unveiling the harm favoritism causes to the human psyche; therefore, as a people, we have to do better, operating in the Spirit of Righteousness without playing pretend with those we claim to love.

- ☐ An unapologetic individual thinks apologizing makes them appear weak, unstable, or a prime pushover.

- ☐ A person who is a user does not care about who they are using as long as they get what they want, when they want it, regardless of who it hurts or gets in the way.

☐ An individual living in a secret or open state of bondage usually seeks to place others in bondage as well. Mainly, this is accomplished through all forms of controlling or withholding tactics to leverage their superficial power to cover up disguised weaknesses.

☐ A person operating in a Spirit of Disobedience usually appears outwardly obedient but self-defiantly rebellious from within. Often enough, this is revealed in their willful recklessness, intentional mistakes, self-sabotage, intentionally rejecting those they desire to control, provoking anger within others to destabilize them mentally or emotionally, causing emotional instability within the one who is holding the rod, intentionally forgetting as an excuse not to do something, and so on.

☐ An out-of-control person does not realize they lack self-control because they get what they want without being questioned. And, if they are questioned, they block, reject, abuse, or traumatize the person who is questioning them, teaching them not to resist or break their system of conveyance to get what they want, when they want it, how they want it, why they want it, and with whom.

By not taking the time to *Query* ourselves, this behavior gets swept under the rug until it unveils itself as a generational curse, spreading throughout our Bloodline until someone steps up to the plate to put an end to it. If not, the Cycle of Seedtime and Harvest will continue to run through our Bloodline as if it is normal. When, in all actuality, it is abnormal, but we do not know it due to some form of Spiritual Blindness, Deafness, or Muteness.

Now, to add insult to injury, when in this state, we will find ourselves blaming, bullying, mistreating, pointing the finger, or pouncing upon others for NOT tolerating our unruliness. Moreover, this state of being will also cause us to mistreat those who outright reject our generational curse in their Bloodline. Listen, this is real, and until we Spiritually Awaken ourselves from our slumber, this Cycle of Conveyance will continue, gripping the lives of the innocent.

Personally, it breaks my heart to have a little innocent child fall prey to this vicious cycle without having a fighting chance to rise above, due to the lack of understanding of 'What' to do, 'Why' they must make the change, 'How' to make it, 'When' to apply it, 'Where' to target, and with 'Whom.' For me, there is no way that I could leave this world without leaving the vital Spiritual Information, Understanding, Tools, and Know-How, giving others a fighting chance to change the trajectory of their Bloodline from negative to positive, evil to good, cursed to Blessed, unjust to just, unrighteous to righteous, wrong to right, and so on.

When dealing with a known or unknown longing from within, we must prepare ourselves to query our psyche. We must extract our 'What' and 'Why' first, giving us a better understanding of what we are dealing with, which branches off to the other issues associated. What is the purpose of knowing this information? It helps us get the whole truth instead of dealing with half-truths or outright half-dealing with issues in need of our wholehearted attention.

Suppose we know 'What' our issues are or 'What' we are feeling. But, we fail to know 'How' to deal with them according to the Standards of the Kingdom. So, we opt to fix them our way. Only to find out it is a temporary fix to a generational situation. What do we do? We must get to the root of whatever or whomever. According to the Heavenly of Heavens, omitting the 'Why' of whatever we are dealing with, known or unknown, makes it harder to regraft, uproot, or reseed, causing the Cycle of Life to repeat itself. At the same time, we continue to become resistant to change.

As It Pleases God®: Book Series

    Here is the deal: If we are not accustomed to honestly *Querying* ourselves, we will naturally revert to pointing the finger, diverting responsibility, shifting blame, rationalizing, justifying, manipulating, or making false accusations to benefit us or our situation. What is the big deal? We are problem-solvers by nature, but for some reason, we have become desensitized to doing so due to worldliness, conditioning, biases, parental-imposed limitations, environmental adaptations, and so on.

    To be clear, regardless of who we are and where we are from, we are truly a Genius in disguise. Why are we not operating as such? First, we do not realize our potential, *As It Pleases God*. Secondly, we do not understand how to properly *Query* ourselves to unveil, expose, or uplift ourselves and others with our Gifts, Calling, Talents, Creativity, or Purpose. Thirdly, we have been taught to suppress our Inner Genius, or we do not know it exists, while lashing out at those who seemingly mastered theirs. By doing so, this behavior suppresses and compounds the layers of debris covering our own. Lastly, we lack the understanding that our inner settings have everything to do with our Mindset, and we cannot opt to please ourselves as if no one matters in the Eye of God!

    As a form of deception, we are quick to point the finger regarding someone else's Level of Relationship with God based on our perception, without using Spiritual Means as a form of discernment. Instead, we attempt to secretly kill their dreams to propel our own or outright discredit them.

    According to the Kingdom, we must build ourselves to build others, to place a Spiritual Seal on our foundational edifices. At the same time, activating the Law of Reciprocity to Spiritually Guard and Protect our own. But what do we do? For some reason, we do the opposite. We take from where we have not sown, tilled, or placed the 'Sweat of our Brow,' while secretly or openly debilitating our brothers and sisters to make ourselves appear better, wiser, and stronger. Meanwhile, in or out of the Kingdom, humility, proactively sharing, nurturing, and helping others make us better, wiser, and stronger.

As It Pleases God®: Book Series

What Spiritual Means should we look for? With all due respect, anyone can pretend to be Heaven Sent, Holy-Ghost-Filled, and Fire-Baptized, Spiritually Anointed, well-versed with scriptures, and so on. But according to the *Unveiled Queries* from the Heavenly of Heavens, our Spiritual Means starts within our human psyche, spreading outwardly. What does this mean? We must examine ourselves first, doing a self-analysis or a checkup from the neck up, while repenting of any hidden cobwebs of deception clouding our sense of good judgment.

How do we go about doing so? First, as a form of Spiritual Formality, we must look for the Fruits of the Spirit and Christlike Character, especially when they are truly our governing factors related to an outward manifestation of primal evidence. Secondly, we must look for the factors of thanksgiving, mercy, compassion, understanding, forgiveness, and repentance. Thirdly, we must consider the level of our proactive giveback, unselfishness, helpfulness, and fairness.

Once accomplished from within, the Holy Spirit will begin to alert us or send red flags to watch out for certain things, and NOT to act upon them. What does this mean? We must pay attention, setting a Spiritual Guard over our Mind, Body, and Soul to avoid being deceived, misled, used, abused, or ostracized by those who contradict the Fruits of the Spirit, Christlike Character, who are knowingly or unknowingly a wolf in sheep's clothing, or those lacking a conscience. Now, here is the deal: This could apply to us as well. Therefore, we should not string our hope or faith along with a bunch of hoopla or lies.

Unbeknown to most, our *Unveiled Queries* are necessary for our walk in the Will of God, according to our Divine Blueprint, *As It Pleases Him*. If they are not done, we become limited, and our *Courage* will take a hit. In the Kingdom, there are specific prerequisites to *Unveil* our hidden motives. What does this mean? We cannot behave like junkyard dogs, thinking God will smile upon this sort of behavior because He will NOT! Actually, He frowns upon unrighteousness, especially if we do not query or work on ourselves to become better and more repentant.

What if we choose not to work on ourselves? We will begin to develop bigger voids, longings, and desires for more of something or someone based upon the lust of the eyes, the lust of the flesh, and the pride of life.

Suppose we do not involve ourselves in the *Unveiled Queries* from within. In this case, we are going to overlook the vital information needed to establish Spiritual Righteousness in the Eye of God. How will we overlook this process? We will operate the way we are accustomed to behaving, or we may whitewash it based on our perception of grace, forgiveness, repentance, and mercy without any form of healing for the human psyche.

Spiritual Whitewashing is prevalent among us, running rampant, seeking to devour us based upon the principles of our worldly perception without incorporating Kingdom Principles, Spiritual Fruits, and Christlike Character. And, according to the Heavenly of Heavens, we must bring a halt to the extermination of the Biblical Principles designed to save our lives and our Bloodline, which were given to us by our Forefathers from the Ancient of Days.

The layout of our charactorial behaviors is woven into the pages of the Bible. Still, we overlook it consistently, using grace as an excuse instead of a form of Spiritual Backup in our time of need. What does this mean? We are less likely to use grace when we are operating consistently with the Fruits of the Spirit and Christlike Character, while using it in areas where we really need it. After all, this keeps us from Spiritually Abusing the systems set in place as a safety net, catching us when we fall short.

And now, with the whitewashing of the use of grace, we do not want to put in the work to become better from the inside out. By doing so, we decline in the positivity of our Mindset while defaulting to the negativity without realizing it. Or, we fall upon grace to avoid the *Unveiled Queries* in dire need of answers, fearing it will expose our true colors. So, my question is, 'Who is hurting whom?'

Furthermore, if we refuse to communicate with ourselves genuinely, it is reflected outwardly, regardless of how well we attempt to mask it. This massive cover-up causes us to engage in deflecting our *Q and A Sessions* with ourselves, thinking our answers reside elsewhere. But in all actuality, we must look within to answer the hard questions we refuse to answer or dig deep for those we do not know to ask. In doing so, it brings us back to the '*What*' and '*Why*' of whatever and with whomever to properly extract the '*How-To*' or '*Know-How*' needed to rise above our worldly ways, getting rid of the superficial fluff.

How do we get rid of the superficial fluff? We must challenge it! When we challenge our negative inner chatter by asking it fact-finding questions in the *What, When, Where, How, Why,* and with *Whom* formation, we position ourselves to contend with or reverse the negatives into positives. Most importantly, it helps us to *Query* the type of fruits or characteristics we are exhibiting as well, allowing us to repent and interject the Fruits of the Spirit and Christlike Character into the equation.

Our psyche will never opt to do this on its own without proper training, nor does it want to be governed by the Holy Spirit. But the truth is, we have the last say in this matter by the *Unveiled Queries* we are having with ourselves, getting to the root of any matter without losing our sense of good judgment. Doing so will cause us to grow in our *Courage* from the inside out and create win-wins, especially when others see defeat.

The *Unveiled Queries* are designed to peel back the layers preventing us from Spiritually Seeing, Hearing, and Speaking the way we were naturally designed according to our Divine Blueprint. From this point onward, we have two choices:

- ☐ Move forward.
- ☐ Remain held back.

We often expect God to do all of our inner work, whereas God is waiting for us to make an effort. Really? Yes, really. If one has not noticed by now, in the Bible, when God corrects, He begins to do so by asking a question, provoking us to think, ponder, remember, or respond. For example, Job 40:6-7 says, *"Then the LORD answered Job out of the whirlwind, and said: Now prepare yourself like a man; I will question you, and you shall answer Me."*

God is not doing this for show; He is letting us know the importance of proactively *Querying* ourselves, allowing us to understand, repent, forgive, and self-correct before Spiritual Correction takes place. Now, if we allow it to get this far, we cannot expect to get a slap on the hand to continue in our folly.

Most often, God will begin the correction process within the human psyche, causing us to fight against ourselves, spreading outwardly, as we make a mess. Therefore, if we experience someone who is blaming their messes on others without assuming responsibility, it should raise red flags regarding things to come.

The oozing of mess does not discriminate. It will mess up or consume anything within its path, similar to an erupting volcano. Furthermore, if we are standing within its reach, it will consume us by default, especially if we do not kindly back up or keep our distance. So, in order to stop the flow of mess, we must invoke some form of clean-up process, starting from the inside out.

Now, to take this a step further, when working on ourselves from the inside out, it is best to involve the Holy Spirit to help in this matter, getting into the crevices of the human psyche that man cannot go or tap into. The deep-rooted elements of trauma, conditioning, biases, or misunderstandings vary from person to person, culture to culture, Bloodline to Bloodline, and so on. Without Divine Intervention, the root must remain hidden until it is adequately *Unveiled* or *Queried*; therefore, what works for one person may not work for another.

According to the Heavenly of Heavens, we cannot equate Spiritual Matters with worldly intervention. In so many words, what originates from the Spirit must be corrected in the Realm of the Spirit. Listed below are a few examples, but not limited to such:

- ☐ Any Bloodline, Birthright, or curse must be dealt with by Spiritual Means.

- ☐ Anything dealing with our Divine Blueprint must be dealt with through Spiritual Means. If not, we are limited to a portion.

- ☐ When we are dealing with our Gifts, Calling, Talents, and Creativity, we must involve the Holy Spirit to enable the Genius from within to come forth. If not, once again, we are functioning at a limited capacity.

- ☐ When dealing with Spiritual Paralysis, we must involve Spiritual Measures to break the yoke, bondage, chain, or whatever is keeping us in this condition.

- ☐ When we use the Fruits of the Spirit, we must involve the Holy Spirit to govern their distribution or the lack thereof.

- ☐ When we exhibit Christlike Character, we must involve Spiritual Principles to maximize our people skills, causing the human psyche to respond on any level and with anyone.

- ☐ In order to receive Divine Revelation, we need to develop a Direct Connect to the Kingdom of God.

- ☐ When dealing with Spiritual Blindness, Deafness, or Muteness, we must involve the Holy Trinity in Unveiling our Spiritual Vision, Understanding, and Language.

- [ ] When developing our Spiritual Instincts to their maximum capacity, we must involve the Holy Trinity.

- [ ] When we are seeking grace, mercy, and forgiveness, we need the Blood of Jesus to cover us in this matter, the Holy Trinity to guide us, and the Word of God to place a Spiritual Seal.

- [ ] When we are REGRAFTING our fruits, we need the Power of the Holy Trinity to assist us in this process.

- [ ] When we seek Divine Protection, we must involve the Holy Trinity when putting on the Whole Armor of God. If not, we will fail to know how to use our Spiritual Weapons in worldly combat or Spiritual Warfare. In my opinion, what good is having the Spiritual Tools without developing the Spiritual *'Know-How'* for their use?

The bottom line is that regardless of where we are in life, we need our Spiritual Portion to enhance and develop ours. Therefore, the *Unveiled Queries* are necessary for the building of our inner man and should not be taken for granted. Nor should we deprive others of their right to *Query* us to develop an understanding of our intents, mindset, or Spiritual Source. What does this mean? In the *Querying* process, we must become transparent, especially if we are working on ourselves on a moment-by-moment basis to become better, wiser, proactive, helpful, and impactful.

To be clear, this does not mean we should allow people to crucify, pounce, or abuse us. It means we should STAND on our Faith, with the Word of God in hand, using the Fruits of the Spirit and Christlike Character to contend with anything or anyone while keeping it moving in the Spirit of Excellence without flinching an inch.

Why do we need to know about STANDING? When walking in a certain Level of Spirituality, the onlookers will ask questions similar to the Queen of Sheba questioning King Solomon. Here is the reference: *"Now when the queen of Sheba heard of the fame of Solomon concerning the name of the LORD, she came to test him with hard questions. She came to Jerusalem with a very great retinue, with camels that bore spices, very much gold, and precious stones; and when she came to Solomon, she spoke with him about all that was in her heart. So, Solomon answered all her questions; there was nothing so difficult for the king that he could not explain it to her."* 1 Kings 10:1-3.

Now, on the other side of the coin, as a Word to the Wise, when the Spirit of Deception comes knocking on our door, trying to throw us off our game, all we need to do is begin to *Query* them, asking fact-finding questions in the same area they are attempting to throw shade. For this reason, we must become experts in asking and answering questions.

But most importantly, we must LISTEN when they think we are not. The only way to ask the best non-interrogating or non-intrusive questions, getting them to contradict what they are judging, is to ask the right questions. What is the purpose of this? It gets them to hear themselves speak about what they have already spoken about without us becoming confrontational. Does it work? Of course, it does! It works on us, especially when we are secretly or openly deceiving ourselves, and it also works on others as well. For example, this is why Psalm 141:3 says, *"Set a guard, O LORD, over my mouth; keep watch over the door of my lips."*

What is the purpose of mastering our ability to have an *Unveiling Query* with ourselves and others? Once again, all of our issues are derived from within the human psyche, spreading outwardly. So, any outward manifestation has resulted from something inward. More importantly, no one is exempt from this, even if we pretend to be perfect or as if we have it all together; it is an illusion. Why? We are a constant work-in-progress, and we must stay in a repentant state of being to rise above anything or anyone besetting us. Plus, it lessens our bounce-back time.

According to scripture, it asks, "*Where do wars and fights come from among you? Do they not come from your desires for pleasure that war in your members?*" James 4:1. What type of wars are we fighting? Listed below are a few types of warring taking place right before our very eyes, yet we are too blind to see the fight in plain sight. We have:

- ☐ War of Lusts.
- ☐ Wars of Murdering.
- ☐ Wars of Coveting.
- ☐ Wars of Lack.
- ☐ Wars of Omission.
- ☐ Wars of Deprivation.
- ☐ Wars of Asking Amiss.
- ☐ Wars of Inappropriate Spending.
- ☐ Wars of Overindulging on Pleasures.
- ☐ Wars of Worldliness.
- ☐ Wars of Enmity.
- ☐ Warring with God Almighty.

Am I pulling for straws here? Absolutely not. Here is the scripture regarding the causation of the inner warring taking place within the human psyche. "*You lust and do not have. You murder and covet and cannot obtain. You fight and war. Yet you do not have because you do not ask. You ask and do not receive, because you ask amiss, that you may spend it on your pleasures. Adulterers and adulteresses! Do you not know that friendship with the world is enmity with God? Whoever therefore wants to be a friend of the world makes himself an enemy of God.*" James 4:2-4.

Are we really cheating ourselves out of our Blessings or Birthrights? Absolutely. The hypocrisy in our attitudes, behaviors, motives, character, fruits, and so on brings about an opening to become Spiritually Sifted. When, in all actuality, we should humble ourselves to resist unrighteousness.

To be clear, this does not mean we will become perfect overnight, but we must submit to the process of drawing near to God. Let us align this with scripture: *"But He gives more grace. Therefore, He says: 'God resists the proud, but gives grace to the humble.' Therefore, submit to God. Resist the devil and he will flee from you. Draw near to God and He will draw near to you. Cleanse your hands, you sinners; and purify your hearts, you double-minded."* James 4:6-8.

Listen, the Unveiled Queries will work on our behalf if we humbly surrender to the process. What type of guarantee do we have? *"Humble yourselves in the sight of the Lord, and He will lift you up."* James 4:10. What are the steps needed in this surrendering process? Listed below are a few steps to take into account, but not limited to such:

- ☐ Do not speak evil of anyone, outside of making a point of reference or alignment for clarification only.

- ☐ Do not defame the Word of God or His Divine Principles.

- ☐ Do not pass judgment on others; however, we are allowed to assess the fruits to determine what or who we are dealing with, but we cannot condemn anyone to Heaven or the Pit, period.

- ☐ Do not forget our Spiritual Responsibilities according to our Divine Blueprint.

- ☐ Do not put materialism over the people, places, and things that money cannot buy.

- ☐ Do not place value in outer manifestations without accounting for what is taking place from within.

- ☐ Do not avoid spending time ignoring the value encapsulated in every moment while doing the right thing now, not later.

- ☐ Do not become arrogant.

- ☐ Do not grumble, complain, fuss, or fight. Instead, we should apply ourselves, using our Gifts, Talents, Calling, and Creativity to fulfill the Will of God for our lives.

- ☐ Do not ignore what displeases God. Thus, involve Him and give thanks in all things, *As It Pleases Him*. Besides, He is the Creator of it all anyway.

- ☐ Do not forget to do good, doing everything in the Spirit of Righteousness with no regrets, while correcting the correctable by repenting, forgiving, being merciful, and extending compassion to all.

- ☐ Do not take anything or anyone for granted while using the Fruits of the Spirit and Christlike Character in all things and with everyone we come in contact with.

Here is where I extracted the above steps from: "*Do not speak evil of one another, brethren. He who speaks evil of a brother and judges his brother, speaks evil of the law and judges the law. But if you judge the law, you are not a doer of the law but a judge. There is one Lawgiver, who is able to save and to destroy. Who are you to judge another? Come now, you who say, 'Today or tomorrow we will go to such and such a city, spend a year there, buy and sell, and make a profit;' whereas you do not know what will happen tomorrow. For what is your life? It is even a vapor that appears for a little time and then vanishes away. Instead, you ought to say, 'If the Lord wills, we shall live and do this or that.' But now you boast in your arrogance. All such boasting is evil. Therefore, to him who knows to do good and does not do it, to him it is sin.*" James 4:11-17.

Whether we desire normal *Courage* or Supernatural *Courage: As It Pleases God*, they are both available to all. Plus, if we are going through any life-changing events, we still have HOPE, and we cannot give up, regardless of how life appears to the naked eye or who is seeking our demise.

According to the Heavenly of Heavens, the time is NOW to place the Holy Trinity at the forefront, make a conscious effort to use the Fruits of the Spirit, and exhibit Christlike Character. Doing so will revamp the Spiritual Trajectory of our lives in ways superseding human reasoning, granting us a ROAR shaking the foundation of this earth, GUARANTEED!

So, if one dares to indulge in my next books, *Spirit to Spirit* and *The Win-Win of Divine Greatness* in the *As It Pleases God: Book Series*, it will grant Supernatural Bliss beyond what one could ever imagine. Many Blessings.

Dr. Y. Bur

www.DrYBur.com

www.ingramcontent.com/pod-product-compliance
Lightning Source LLC
Chambersburg PA
CBHW071423160426
43195CB00013B/1785